The LANCASHIRE WEATHER BOOK

Len Markham

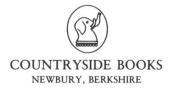

COUNTRYSIDE BOOKS
NEWBURY, BERKSHIRE

First Published 1995
© Len Markham 1995

COUNTRYSIDE BOOKS
3 Catherine Road
Newbury, Berkshire

ISBN 1 85306 351 7

06634124

With thanks to Tom
(an archival mole who has won his spurs)

Front Cover: Blackburn Road, Darwen, July 1964.

Back Cover: Blackpool, February 1990.
(Blackpool Gazette and Herald Ltd.)

Designed by Mon Mohan

Produced through MRM Associates Ltd., Reading
Typeset by Paragon Typesetters, Queensferry, Clwyd
Printed by Woolnough Bookbinding Ltd., Irthlingborough

FOREWORD

Drenched by Atlantic-sodden clouds, Lancashire enjoys the climatic reputation of a sponge – odes and humorous ditties proliferating in sarcastic tribute to leaden skies and an abundance of rain. But such inclement weather, I can say with some conviction, has made this county great. The port of Liverpool might yet be a creek but for a dreadful storm in 1570 which destroyed its haven and sowed, according to the eminent historian Baines, 'the germ of its commercial greatness.' And far from being a disadvantage, the proponderance of moist airs stimulated the development of the inland economy, the atmosphere giving perfect conditions for the spinning of cotton, an industry as synonymous with Lancashire as the raindrop.

Statistically, however, this bonny county belies its reputation. Manchester, with average annual rainfall of between 30 and 35 inches, compares favourably with any city in the north, whilst fabled Southport has long surpassed many of its east coast rivals in the sunshine stakes. But the cantankerous English weather is no respecter of norms and Lancashire has, over the years, experienced a catalogue of extremes, documented together, here, for the first time.

In this book are all your soggy yesterdays – floods and tempests galore, lightning strikes, blizzards and, for good measure, occasional earthquakes, tornadoes and droughts. Derived from ancient journals, personal diaries, weather station forecasts, scientific analyses, newspaper archives and a host of personal reminiscences, these accounts, matched by some exceptional photographs, will I hope, make for exciting reading.

Coming from the north, I am well familiar with northern weather. In the kaleidoscopic nature of meteorology, it tends towards the black. However, things are looking up for both

New Brighton promenade takes a pounding on 27th February, 1990.
(Liverpool Daily Post & Echo)

counties. Over the last 60 years or so, gradual improvements in our atmospheric conditions, as a result of industrial and domestic electrification and the conversion to gas, have markedly cut emissions and pollution. The benefits have been transparent – reduced fog and smog, less oppressive summers, more winter frosts and, so they say, burgeoning sun. May I ask that all sightings of such UFOs be reported to the nearest police station?

Len Markham

(Above) Maghull misery – the heavy rains of October 1994 brought chaos to the low lying areas between the river Alt and the Leeds & Liverpool canal. (Liverpool Daily Post & Echo)
(Below) Part of the pier structure and the frozen sea at Southport in 1963. (Southport Visitor)

Promenade damage at Blackpool, 1879.
(John Hannavy Picture Collection)

CONTENTS

A doorstep in Manchester in the winter of 1991/2. (E. Zmronge)

LANCASHIRE...OR WHAT'S LEFT OF IT!

Apart from an outcrop of red sandstone at Cockersand Abbey, there are no solid coastal landforms between Heysham and the Wirral peninsula, the comparatively soft alluviums, peats, sands and shingles being readily eroded by riverine floods and the constant attention of waves and weather. Over geological time Lancashire's western fringes have been worn away. Only in recent times have sea defences halted the process in particularly important and vulnerable areas and over the centuries whole villages have been engulfed and lost without trace.

One of the earliest catastrophes may have been the loss of the Roman settlement of Portus Sentantiorum on an assumed site near the Wyre outfall. Traditions also speak of the villages of Waddum Thorpe south of Lytham, in a location now covered by the Ribble estuary, and of sea-deep Singleton Thorpe west of Blackpool.

THE WEATHER IN THE EARLY YEARS

Year Dot: It Beats Stand Pipes!

'There is a tradition, in the neighbourhood of Grimsargh, near Preston, to the effect that during some drought, in the olden time, a gigantic dun cow appeared and gave an almost unlimited supply of milk, which saved the inhabitants from death. An old woman – of the witch fraternity, I suspect – however, with the view to obtaining from the beast more than the usual number of pails-full, milked the cow with a sieve, riddle, or colander, which, of course, never became full, as the precious liquid passed through the orifices into the vessel below. When full, the latter was replaced by an empty one of a similar character. The tradition adds that the cow either died of grief or sheer exhaustion . . . A locality is still pointed out, named "Cow Hill", where gossips aver that, in relatively recent times, the huge bones of the said cow were disinterred.' (Charles Hardwick, 1872)

1294: Mersey Mud

According to the ancient chronicle of St Werburgh, vast tracts of cultivated land alongside the Mersey were abandoned to floods.

1543: Bridge across the Mersey

The timber bridge over the river at Warrington was swept away in a catastrophic flood. An appeal was made by the local bishop for help with the costly work of reconstruction. Such was the regularity of bridge loss to the frequent Mersey spates that his holiness specified stone.

29th March 1461: Red Rose Vanquished in Blizzard

One of the most momentous days in British military history broke cold and grey, a mischievous wind fanning the camp fires of two opposing armies. On Palm Sunday morning 50,000 Lancastrians and 60,000 Yorkists mustered on Towton Moor near Tadcaster in Yorkshire to contest the bloodiest battle ever fought on English soil.

The hostilities commenced mid-morning as the wind freshened and snow began to fall from a darkening sky. Taking advantage of the blinding storm which flew full in the faces of the Lancastrians, the Yorkist bowmen unleashed furious showers of arrows and then retreated, their tactical manoeuvres going unseen under the curtain of snow. The Lancastrians, in turn, emptied their quivers, but the arrows fell short. And then the Yorkists advanced again and delivered another volley of death.

Hand to hand fighting was joined, the carnage of sword, bill and axe staining the snow crimson. The Cock Beck ran red with blood and the mêlée continued unabated for 10 hours, the warriors fighting 'as if the battle was the Gate of Paradise'. With the arrival of reinforcements, fortunes swung in favour of the white rose and the Yorkists declared a victory, hacking off the heads of the vanquished as grisly souvenirs. Upwards of 37,000 soldiers were killed.

12th December 1553: Morecambe Maelstrom

A tremendous storm badly damaged Walney Island in Morecambe Bay. The onslaught of wind and waves may have expunged the remnants of Herte village, and it is said that the settlement of Crivelton was also swept away.

1565: A Marvellioust Storm

In Liverpool, 'about ten or eleven o'clock last Sunday night suddenly sprung and rose the marvellioust and terriblest storm of wind and weather that continued above six hours or little less as well upon land as water to the great hurt of ... their houses, barns, and wind mills.' Loaded ships embarking for Ireland were described as 'all charged with great horses, all fine apparell and other treasure ...' (Liverpool Town Books)

1580: Black Death

The deadly effects of the plague in Manchester were worsened by bad weather and a consequential poor harvest.

THE SEVENTEENTH CENTURY

1616: The 'Lambards Flood'

The inundation of Manchester, known in history as the 'Lambards Flood' completely devastated the old town, the river Irwell rising by 'several yards' in the course of a few hours. Frantic men were reported to have stood upon Salford Bridge 'ladling up water with a little piggin'.

16th May 1634: ...Storm and Trouble

'The greatest news from the country is of a huge pack of witches which are lately discovered in Lancashire, wherof 'tis said 19 are condemned, and that there are at least 60 already discovered, and yet daily there are more revealed: there are divers of them of good ability, and they have done much harm, I hear it is suspected that they had a hand in raising the great storm, wherein his Majesty (Charles I) was in so great danger at sea in Scotland.' (Sir William Pelham, in a letter to Lord Conway)

March 1643: Gale Force?

During the Civil War a Spanish warship was blown ashore at the mouth of the river Wyre in a gale. In peril, the crew fired a signal

'Monstrously large hailstones'. (Derby Evening Telegraph)

cannon for three days in an attempt to summon help. Eventually, local people realised the plight of the seamen and plucking up courage they rowed out and led the vessel to safety.

Further afield, rumours about the *Santa Ana*, a troopship bound for the Spanish Netherlands, were rife. Memories of the Armada fuelled fears of invasion, although some Parliamentarians suggested that the ship brought reinforcements to aid the Royalist cause. Stirred into action, they despatched 400 infantrymen to apprehend the ship and her strategically important complement of cannon. They were almost beaten to the spoils by the Royalist commander Lord Derby who reached the stricken vessel first and left her in flames. However, the ordnance was retrieved and taken to Lancaster Castle. Conjecture about the mission of the Spanish ship remains.

30th July 1662: Hailstones as Big as Apples

'About four o'clock that day in the afternoon, was a Dreadful Thunder and Lightning for a long time together, and about it, fell a great shower of Hail in a terrible tempest. Hailstones were as big as ordinary apples, some say nine inches compass; one stone that I took up was above four inches, after it had thawed in my hand. The hail broke all our glass windows westward, we have not one quarril [pane] whole on that side; and so it is with most of the houses in and about the town. It hath cut off all the ears of our standing corn, so that most fields that were full of excellent barley and other grain are not worth reaping . . . It hath shaken the apple trees, and in some places bruised the apples in pieces and cut boughs from trees. All (especially the ignorant) were much terrifeid, thinking it had been the day of Judgment.' (The Reverend Nathaniel Heywood, Vicar of Ormskirk)

1677: Rain Gauger

Richard Townley, the famous mathematician of Townley Hall near Burnley was the first known regular observer of rainfall in England, beginning his detailed record keeping in January 1677. He described his collecting apparatus to the Royal Society in 1694, 'a Round Tunnel of 12 inches diameter.' This receptacle was kept in a ground floor chamber and was joined by means of an elbow passing through a window to a nine yards long vertical leaden pipe stretching up to the battlements. From his observations Townley deduced that Lancashire was generally wetter than parts of neighbouring Yorkshire, recognising that precipitation here on the western slopes of the Pennines is influenced by the prevailing south and south-westerly winds, 'the general winds of this part of the world'. He colourfully added 'the clouds are often stopt and broken and fall upon us.'

1684: Deep and Crisp

After a bone-shattering frost, ground froze to a depth of 'three quarters of a yard' at Northenden near Manchester.

1688: Weather Damage Tops Three Pounds

A catastrophic storm in Bolton damaged the old bridge at the foot of Church Bank. Two bills were presented for the subsequent repair. One was for £1 1s 6d, the other for £2 3s 0d.

THE EIGHTEENTH CENTURY

14th June 1718: Tornado!

According to the records of the Tornado Research Organisation, a devastating tornado struck a hillside at Emott Moor near Colne, gouging out a 7 ft deep trench to bedrock depth. The accompanying sound of 'an unusual noise in the air' terrified a gang of labourers who were working nearby. Over half a mile long and up to 60 ft wide, the chasm quickly filled with rainwater as an aerial waterspout burst.

1740: Cold Feet

Ice was reported 'two feet thick' on the tidal Lune at Lancaster.

1746: High Wyre

Continuous heavy rain caused the swollen waters of the river Wyre to pour into the churchyard at Garstang. The church was severely damaged. Demolition was contemplated and designs were commissioned for a replacement structure. On closer examination, however, it was realised that the assessment of structural instability had been over pessimistic and the church was repaired.

13th June 1749: Barmy Summer

A snow covering extending below altitudes of 500 ft, was widely reported on the Pennines.

29th July 1768: A Ship Comes In

Liverpool was battered by a storm of intense violence. Many houses in the lower part of the town were inundated. Dozens of vessels were wrecked and the bowsprit of the *Wheel of Fortune* was driven through the window of a dwelling in James Street.

1776: Bad Vibrations

Manchester is subject to earthquake shocks as a consequence of its proximity to the Pendleton fault. In 1776, so strong were the convulsions that church bells were set ringing across the town.

1777: The End Is Nigh

Sandwich-boarded street walkers ran for cover as an earthquake struck Bacup in September.

1784 – 5: Gnawing Cold

Thousands of workers across Lancashire were thrown out of work following the imposition of a tax on linen and cotton goods. The mass lay-offs coincided with a poor harvest and a bitter five months long winter. Temperatures plunged to 18 degrees below freezing point and many people died of starvation. Subsequent bad weather in the following summer again reduced crop yields and the price of bread soared, leading to rioting, machine wrecking and factory burning.

A blow out in Old Hall Street, Liverpool, 27th April 1990. (Liverpool Daily Post & Echo)

1794: Lighting Up Time

The spectacle of the aurora borealis was enjoyed by Lancashire sky-watchers on six occasions during the year.

18th January 1795: Dryer Brigade

The New Exchange building in Water Street, Liverpool caught fire in the early morning during a period of intense frost 'which sealed up the water pipes'. The building was completely destroyed.

GENERAL
HAIL STORM INSURANCE
SOCIETY.

Head Office, Norwich.
London Office, 26, Birchin Lane.

PATRONS.

THE DUKE OF NORFOLK	THE EARL OF LEICESTER
THE EARL OF ALBEMARLE	THE LORD WALSINGHAM
THE EARL OF ABERGAVENNY	THE LORD COLBORNE
THE EARL OF ORFORD	THE HON. W. R. ROUS
THE LORD STAFFORD	THE HON. ADMIRAL IRBY
THE LORD BAYNING	SIR T. H. E. DURRANT, BART.
SIR EDMUND BACON, BART.	SIR W. J. H. B. FOLKES, BART.
SIR W. B. PROCTOR, BART.	SIR E. H. K. LACON, BART.
SIR CHARLES M. CLARKE, BART.	SIR W. FOSTER, BART.
EDMOND WODEHOUSE, ESQ. M P.	W. L. W. CHUTE, ESQ. M. P.
H. N. BURROUGHES, ESQ. M. P.	B. SMITH, ESQ. M. P.
EDWARD FELLOWES, ESQ. M. P.	J. B. S. BRADFIELD, ESQ.
R. SANDERSON, ESQ. M. P.	H. D'ESTERRE HEMSWORTH, ESQ.
EDWARD BAGGE, ESQ.	JOHN LONGE, ESQ.
T. R. BUCKWORTH, ESQ.	MAJOR LOFTUS
J. T. MOTT, ESQ.	&c. &c. &c.

DIRECTORS.

SAMUEL BIGNOLD, ESQ.	ROBERT PRATT, ESQ.
JOHN WRIGHT, ESQ.	THOMAS SALTER, ESQ.
JOHN SKIPPER, ESQ.	JAMES NEAVE, ESQ.
F. J. BLAKE, ESQ.	JOHN CANN, ESQ.
ROGER KERRISON, ESQ.	J. HILLING BARNARD, ESQ.

BANKERS.	SECRETARIES.
Messrs. GURNEYS & BIRKBECK.	C. S. GILMAN & E. C. MORGAN.

The great destruction of property by the Hail Storm on the 9th of August, 1843, which appears to have spread ruin and desolation amongst the Framers and Gardeners in many parts of the Kingdom, more particularly in the Counties of Norfolk, Suffolk, Essex, Cambridge, Bedford, Oxford, and Hertford, has proved the absolute necessity of adopting measures for securing individuals against the pecuniary losses attending these terrific visitations.

Experience has shewn, that Hail Storms, for many years past, have been of more frequent occurrence than formerly. In several cases only partial losses have been sustained, yet there are many instances where farmers and others have had to lament the total destruction of their property ; and although large subscriptions have been raised, yet none sufficiently ample to place these sufferers in their former position, whilst many persons, whose

Insurance policy issued at Cheadle in 1844.

20

WEATHER DIARY 1787–1830

The following previously unpublished extracts are from the remarkable weather diary of William Rowbottom of Oldham. A knowledgeable amateur meteorologist and naturalist, he has left us an illuminating, sometimes humorous and often joyous commentary on 18th and 19th century life.

'1787: The latter end of June 1787 to the latter end of August 1787 was one of the wettest Hay Harvest ever Known . . . It rained the Greatest part of those days . . . November 5th 1787 was one of the most tremendos Night of rain . . . Nothing could stop the Vellocity of the water for it sweept down all bridges etc before it at Chaderton hall it burst all the fish ponds in the srubbery Salford bridge was taken and a man was drowned as he was standing looking over one side of it.

October 1795: Fine Wheather wich begun August 25th and Continues til October 7th the space of 43 days wich was the finest Harvest Ever Known the air was very warm and at some times was very Sultry and hot all sorts of insects and reptiles as if a Second Sumer was Comenced and the Earth seemd as if She sent forth a double portion of vegetation the Brooks for lack of rain where low and the fishes as Sportive and Active as if in June or July the Birds by the uncomonness of the wheather joined all products of Nature with their melodious Notes wich would have Convinced the most rigid atheiest of the Blesings of the Almighty God, it should not be forgot that fleas where very numerous and very much anoyed poor people in bed ith night.

June 1806: The Excesive Drought still Continues and this morning it was such a Strong Frost that the ground was wite over and water become so Exceeding Scarse that Even pit water is Sold a halfpenny a Burn in and about Oldham . . .

2nd May 1809: Oldham fair a cold day but a deal of company a deal of recruiting . . . Oh the Baneful Efects of this Acursed War.

25th August 1810: . . . was Oldham Rushbearing Sauterday . . . in all nine Rushcarts . . . it was Exalent weather . . . High spending and much fighting.

31st March 1811: Fine Spring such as was never known Before by the Oldest person Living . . . all sorts of Blossoms making Rapid apearances Flowers and vegetation in uncomon Fordwadness and the Flaxfinch, the Goldfinch, the Red Robin, the Hedge Sparrow, the Sky lark, the Titlark and the Stump wren vie with Each other to welcome in this fine spring and the Lady smock is in full Bloom.

31st August 1811: . . . was Oldham Rushbearing Sauterday a fine day till towards night when it turned to Rain there was but few Company and in consequence of the times there was but only one Rushcart . . . they took the Rushes Back so that on Rushbearing Sunday there was not a Single Rush in Oldham Church to preserve old peoples feet from cold during the winter.

1st January 1814: . . . Sauterday was an Extreem fine Day the sky being serene and clear and as warm as in April by the Recent victorys of the Allies over the French.

9th February 1814: . . . During the Last hard frost the ground in the Church Yard Oldham on the north East Quater was froze Twenty Eight Inches Deep was proved by the Sexton in makeing graves and during the late storm a very Large Quantity of Fish have Been Killed and a Deal of Birds have shared the same unhappy fate, several field fares have been picked up in this neighbourhood.

3rd July 1814: . . . this day being Sunday prayers were offered up for Rain in Oldham Church.

26th August 1815: Was Oldham Wakes Sauterday in the forenoon some Thunder and Rain but in the afternoon very fine there were eight Rushcarts and one Rush waggon . . . On Sunday an Exalent fine day and much company . . . on Monday a fine day and Two Rushcarts and Grand parading with the nimps [nymphs!] and swayns [swans!] . . . a very superb and grand Banner was brought from Chadderton and Displayed with Great pomp on Tuesday a fine day on Wednesday a horse race for a Saddle a Bridle and wip . . . on Friday a foot race for a Bakestone and a peck of Meal . . . upon the whole it as Been the most grand and splendid wakes wich as Been in the memory of the oldest person living private familys Brewed a Deal and uncomon Deal of Drinking at the ale Houses . . . it was an absolute fact that seventy three head of Horned Cattle Besides sheep lambs and Calfes where slaugtered and dispenced with . . .

1st January 1819: The year 1819 begun on Fryday wich was a very fine warm day but a little misty as for Cristmas Cheer there was but little to be seen and poor people scarsely left off working trade is very brisk but wages low and all the nessessarys of Life so very Dear.

7th September 1820: there was a great Ecleips on the Sun.

1st December 1821: Most Tremendous High wind comenced at an early hour last night was very astonishing high this morning . . . the shiping on the Scotish and Irish coasts suffered very much as well as on the Lanchashire and Yorkshire coasts it blew down a deal of houses in Liverpool Manchester and other places a deal of unfortunate beings perished in the ruins of Oldham . . . it blew down several new built buildings uninhabited blew down the primitive methodist or Ranters Chappel blew down the large chimney at Mr Curzons factory wich fell upon a cottage house and buried the family in its ruins some had limbs broke but happily no lives where lost . . .'

23

THE NINETEENTH CENTURY

January 1802: Lights Out

Hurricane force winds toppled a factory chimney in Manchester, destroying three houses and mortally injuring a woman and a child. Falling masonry also claimed the lives of two pedestrians. Fearing further casualties, the authorities closed the theatre. City streets were blacked out as gas lamps were contorted by the blast and their flames snuffed out. In a local park, 600 trees were either snapped in two or uprooted.

4th May 1804: 'Shiver Me Timbers!'

'At Bolton and vicinity, the people experienced a most dreadful tornado, and it is supposed that a waterspout must have burst, the river Irwell having swelled to so great a height as to sweep away many buildings and large quantities of household furniture. The duration of the storm was upwards of two hours. At Hulton Park a ball of fire fell with such force as to split in shivers and tear up an ash tree, which had long been admired for its strength and beauty. Several bridges were thrown down.' (Annual Register)

6th August 1809: A Thunderbolt in Swinton

'. . . after repeated peals of distant and approaching thunder in the lower country, the heavens became suddenly enveloped in thick darkness; and it was thought prudent to open all the doors of the house, as the best preparation for receiving the expected storm. No sooner was this done, than a tremendous explosion occurred; . . .'

This explosion, a tremendous thunderbolt, hit the house of Mr Elias Chadwick at Swinton. The 'electric fluid' bodily spun the old gentleman and a visitor round without injury, then went on to demolish most of an 11 ft high brick built cistern in the garden, sending an avalanche of debris estimated at 26 tons in weight crashing to the ground. 'Immediately after the explosion, rain fell in a torrent, deluging for a moment everything around it; and for a few minutes the air in the nearer parts of the house was offensively smoky and sulphureous.'

5th December 1822: A Briny Blow

After a violent westerlies-driven storm, the eminent Manchester scientist John Dalton FRS detected traces of salt on his window panes. He immediately chemically analysed a sample of rain gauge water and found it contained salt. 'There can be but one opinion as to the cause,' he determined, 'it must be brought by the violent impetuosity of the wind activity upon the spray from the tumultous waves of the ocean.'

11th June 1833: Dire Nights in Blackpool

Eleven ships were sunk and many more were left floundering off shore as a devastating summer storm rampaged off Blackpool. Dawn revealed a scene of maritime carnage – spars and decking smashed to matchwood and diverse cargoes littering the shore.

The crew of a Lerwick sloop had a miraculous escape in heavy seas. Guided by candlelight shining from a window in the old Gynn Inn the ship's master managed to guide his craft through a narrow opening between the cliffs to safety. The elated and chastened crew gave thanks for their deliverance at a local church, much in contrast to a rescued Irish crew who celebrated in drunken debauchery.

Events of New Year's Eve ended that fateful year with a bang. Heavy seas inundated lower Blackpool, demolishing walls and buildings and swamping fields and meadows. The subsiding waters revealed a heartbreaking conglomeration of sludge, bricks, sticks, broken slates and personal belongings.

1839: Gale of the Century

Once in every epoch, one weather incident eclipses all others. In Lancashire's meteorological hall of infamy for the 19th century, it was the hurricane of the 6th and 7th of January in this year that took centre stage.

An 108 page account of the disaster records the graphic details, 'it became a perfect hurricane soon after midnight. It continued to blow in this dreadful manner for many hours without a moment's cessation, sweeping down chimneys and chimney pots, tearing up slates by the thousands, snapping in pieces large trees, casting down thick walls, driving vessels on shore and spreading death and destruction on every side . . .' Across the county, from Liverpool to the boundary with Yorkshire and beyond, the wind brought untold misery.

In Liverpool there was not a street, nor hardly a berthed ship left undamaged from the 'elemental war which had raged during the night.' Many commercial and industrial premises in the port were also badly damaged. The North Shore Cotton Factory had its roof and two upper storeys torn away and tons of cotton fibre

Snow bowlers . . . mass hysteria of the hatted classes. The Liverpool Exchange, 5th January 1854. (City of Liverpool Public Libraries)

were scattered over a wide area. In Great Mersey Street, cotton festooned the roadside 'which appeared as during a snow storm and the hedges and trees from thence to Everton afforded an excellent imitation of hoar frost, so delicately was the carded cotton sprinkled upon every object obstructing its passage through the troubled air.' Such was the ferocity of the storm that the sails of a windmill in Oil Street were ripped off and a 100 yard section of a wall at the Kirkdale Gaol was demolished, a detachment of police being despatched to guard the breach.

Elsewhere, 300 trees were bowled over in the woods of Hale Hall, and the Salt Works in Garstang and the Vitriol Factory in Wigan were both 'much injured'. Salt spray was driven inland over a considerable distance and salt crystals encrusted shrubs and trees in St Helens. The coast north of the Mersey was a scene of utter devastation. A stricken merchantman, the *Pennsylvania*, was cast ashore in Blackpool and vast quantities of tobacco, bales of cotton and cloth and diverse crates and pots made easy pickings for hordes of wreckers.

1851: These Barometers Suck Blood

Recruited for their forecasting powers, leeches were exhibited at the Great Exhibition, where a Dr Merryweather displayed a contrivance for predicting the weather. Confined in bottles of water, the little fellows gave notice of impending tempests by ringing a bell! The eminent doctor advised the government to establish leech-warning stations along the Lancashire coast and elsewhere. His suggestions were not taken up.

5th March 1860: Weather Hoax

Before the advent of videos and disaster movies, Lancastrians would satisfy their passion for calamity watching by visiting Blackpool! Low lying and constantly vulnerable to flooding from adverse winds and high seas, Lancashire's premier resort often made news, attracting many sightseers. Crowds of people whose curiosities were roused by lurid eye-witness accounts of devastation and dire prognostications of inundations in such newspapers as the *Preston Pilot*, converged to enjoy the adventures of baling out and rooftop rescues. Entertainment had never been so cheap! Mobilised by a particularly graphic leader in March 1860, they came by the cartload, scores of mill workers impelled by the prospects of high tides and mayhem. But instead of the promised flood they got only an average neap and blue skies. The inlanders were livid and many returned home convinced they were victims of a commercially inspired hoax. 'Their great tide were nowt i' th' world but an arrant sell, getten up by lodgin' heawse keepers, an' railway chaps, an' newspapper folk, an' sich like wastril devils, a-purpose to bring country folk to th' wayter-side and hook brass eawt o' their pockets...'

27th November 1860: Weather Sickness

At a meeting of the Manchester Literary and Philosophical Society a controversial paper was discussed, its author, the eminent doctor Thomas Moffat MD, alleging a causal link between inclement weather and bad health. The paper, 'On the prevalence of certain forms of disease in connection with Hail and Snow Showers, and the Electric condition of the Atmosphere', stimulated a lively debate. After two years' research, Moffat observed that 'an intimate connexion existed between falls of snow and hail and diseases of the nervous centres, such as apoplexy, epilepsy, paralysis and vertigo . . .' Commenting on the effects of the gales between the 21st and the 30th October 1859 (in one of which the *Royal Charter* was lost) he noted that 'other forms of disease accompany such atmospheric conditions, such as premature uterine action, epistaxis and diarrhoea with vomiting and cramps.' So called 'negative electricity' was implicated as a contributing factor to these and other ailments. Although ridiculed by many in his day, some of Moffat's assertions have since been proved correct.

16th and 17th November 1866: The Great Flood

This, the most catastrophic weather-responsible disaster ever to afflict Manchester and Salford, caused widespread and terrible damage to property, the extent of the devastation covering an area in excess of 1,100 acres.

Torrential and persistent rain saturated the inadequate drainage capacity of the local watercourses and rivers, the flow rate in the principal conduit – the Irwell – being, at its height, 133 times greater than normal, a colossal 42,000 tons of water per minute tearing through the built-up area and swamping everything in its path.

'. . . there extended one huge lake of turbid water', noted one commentator, 'rushing irresistibly along, and carrying with it in its course everything which it was capable of rooting up or dislodging from its place. It was a truly magnificent sight to those who could from some point of safety stand and take in the panorama of seething waters which lay stretched out before them. But to those who had life and property at stake it was a day of disaster and never ceasing anxiety and dread. In Broughton Lane, and in many other places, the inhabitants might be seen sailing about from house to house in boats and on rafts, and, in fact, upon anything that would float and carry them to some place of security. In many dwellings the water was not only in the cellars and in the living rooms, but might be seen rising up into the bedrooms. Hundreds of families were crowded together in the attics and upper rooms of their houses and cottages, looking with alarm at the water as it mounted higher and higher, lapping against the stairs and cutting off any retreat from their watery prison.'

The inexorable tide carried away everything in its path – entire bridges, whole rows of cottages and flotsam of every description.

'Imagine seeing a dead pig, a family group of cocks and hens perched disconsolately on an old hen coop, in company with a host of miscellaneous articles of all shapes and sizes, household and otherwise; dog-kennels, trees, bandboxes, furniture of all descriptions, hats, wooden boxes and floating crockery, all rushing wildly along and at times jostling and falling foul one of another, as if they were hurrying on and away from some relentless foe who was driving them to destruction, and from whom they were powerless to escape.'

Every available craft, anything that would float, was pressed into service to rescue the marooned victims of the flood. Numerous pleasure boats were carted from the Belle Vue Gardens to facilitate rescues in the Lower Broughton district, and there was heroic action in Broughton Road, Strangeways, Camp Street,

Bury New Road and elsewhere. Many boat loads of people were ferried to the sanctuary of the Town Hall in Duke Street. One stalwart cab proprietor by the name of John Youd did sterling work and 'made many journeys through the water with the "fares" perched on the top of his cab. People wondered that his horse did not shy, but it turned out that this particular animal had pulled bathing machines in and out of the water at Blackpool previously.'

When the waters subsided, housewives and business owners counted the cost of ruination, the total value of the destruction being calculated at over £100,000. This was bad enough but the after effects were even worse. 'The damp got into the walls and the foundations of the houses, and for years hardly a dry healthy habitation could be found where the waters had full play. Sickness and a high death rate were, of course, only a natural consequence, and newcomers avoided Lower Broughton almost like a plague spot. As may readily be supposed, property owners had a very bad time of it; tenants had to be tempted with exceptionally low rents, which I fear would be counterbalanced by bad health and increased doctors bills.'

1872: Licentious Weather

'The young people of Spotland, in the parish of Rochdale, are yet in the habit of assembling on the hill sides on the first Sunday in May, and exchanging congratulations on the return of spring. They drink to each others health in liquor supplied by the pure mountain streamlets . . . No doubt some genuine love-making, as well as much licentiousness, has resulted from the observance of such ceremonies . . .' (Charles Hardwick)

13th July 1872: Flood Exhumes Corpses

In just 48 hours, Manchester was deluged with its normal monthly quota of rain. The obelisk erected in Peel Park to

Blackpool pier demolished by storm, 1879.
(John Hannavy Picture Collection)

commemorate the memorable flood of 1866 was swamped. The greatest damage was inflicted, however, by the raging Medlock. It rose 12 ft. Several bridges were washed away and the cemetery wall in Phillips Park was demolished, allowing the torrent to scour out the grisly contents of scores of graves. In Ancoats the water rose to bedroom height and terrified householders had to be rescued by raft. The dramatic scenes provided the inspiration for the opening chapter of the famous book *The Manchester Man*.

6th July 1881: Killer Storm

A wild and furious lightning storm burst over Bacup and Rossendale. But the pyrotechnics were the least of the problems. Heavy and prolonged rain brought catastrophic flooding and in Bacup there was a fearful loss of life. As a little girl was being carried across Burnley Road to safety by her grandfather, a raging current took them both away. The child's lifeless body was found some hours later in Henrietta Street, a half mile distant. In Dawson's Cottages a woman drowned in her cellar abode after a dramatic rescue attempt by her husband. A third victim was swept away after leaving the back door of the Waterloo Hotel. The poor woman's cries for help as she floated down the narrow alley were described as heart-rending by the neighbours. Damage to the local textile industry was catastrophic. About 400 looms were submerged in the Irwell Mill alone. The storm also played havoc in Accrington where the driver of the mail cart from Burnley to Accrington was seriously hurt.

16th November 1895: A Bit of a Dampener . . . for some

On this busy Saturday all Bacupians were in party mood. The festivities were set in train at noon by the annual chrysanthemum

One boiler was lit to keep the captain warm. Frost freezes the Mersey, 1881. (Watercolour by E Beattie, City of Liverpool Public Libraries)

show, followed in the afternoon by an important football match at West View. In the evening scores of people enjoyed an 'At Home' at Wesley Place and a 'Cake and Apron' celebration at South Street. Persistent rain failed to dampen the early enthusiasm of the crowds, but between 1 o'clock and 2 o'clock storm clouds brought massive flooding of the lower lying areas of the town. Forest Mill, Throstle Mill, Plantation Mill, India Mill and Springholme Mill were all 'invaded' and the Bull's Head Hotel 'experienced lively times'. A number of its barrels of ale simply floated away. Mysteriously, they were never recovered.

1895: 'How On Earth Did We Keep Warm?'

Nearly 50 years on, one Lancashire lass recalled her frozen childhood.

'How did we – females in cotton nightdresses, males in cotton nightshirts – fail to dread the moment when noses and hands should be brought gingerly from under the bedclothes to meet the icy air? In those days not only was the very name of central heating unknown where I lived but also there were no gas fires, far less electric ones . . . In our house we must have had, so I calculate, five coal fires going regularly with two extra ones going less regularly. Then in the day time we wore "flannel next the skin" and woollen stockings, and, in the case of girls, a couple of petticoats at least, not to mention various other garments . . . I have a memory of breaking the ice in my bath. I never missed my cold bath and never was pusillanimous enough to add tepid water, loved my sugarless porridge – as long as it hadn't "knots" in it – and became rosy instead of blue with the cold . . . ' (C.C. Fraser)

19th Century Spits and Spots

1802: On the 21st January, driven by a 'hurricane', an enormous tide engulfed Liverpool docks. The spire of the 1,000 year old Sefton church lost five ft to the wind. At Pendleton near Clitheroe, a mill chimney came crashing down.

1811: A hailstorm in Bury on the 28th June destroyed several thousand ft of glass.

1814–15: On the eve of her marriage to a local surgeon, a distraught Miss Lavinia Robinson, the 'Manchester Ophelia', disappeared from her Bridge Street home. Her body was eventually discovered in the Irwell near the Mode Wheel, the persistent frost and ice-covered river having hidden her corpse for over two months.

1821: Parts of Lancashire were visited by a violent hailstorm. The hailstones came to earth with such velocity that panes of bull's eye glass were broken in exposed windows.

Ice on the Mersey, 1895. (City of Liverpool Public Libraries)

1822: The river Ribble 'affords sources of amusement to the young men of Preston – fishing, bathing, skating and sailing...each resorted to by votaries of these healthful and innocent pleasures. But a melancholy event, arising out of the incautious use of one of them ought to be a perpetual warning against persons venturing in boats upon the water without the requisite skill to manage them. On the 24th April, four fine youths embarked in a small sail-boat; after amusing themselves for some time, a sudden gust of wind upset their boat in the middle of the river, a little below Penwortham Bridge, and they were all drowned before assistance could be afforded them...'

1823: The lower slopes of the Pennines were snow covered on the 5th June.

1830: Many mills in Oldham and district ceased production on the 28th June as a consequence of a violent electrical storm. At Castle Mill near Oldham, lightning passed through 'three thick floors and escaped by a door.' At Tonge Lane, 2½ miles west of the town, hailstones destroyed a vast quantity of gooseberries. The storm also wreaked havoc in Hollinwood, Shaw, Royton and Greenacres Moor.

1832: The advent of cold winter weather brought about a decline in the county death rate from cholera. Across Britain the disease killed 32,000 people in 1831 and 1832.

1833: The old year ended with a bang in Salford where a chimney was bowled over in a gale on New Year's Eve.

1834: On July 30th a tremendous thunderstorm did much damage in Manchester. A thunderbolt killed two men at Newton Heath and a woman was fatally struck down at Prestwich.

1835: Teacups trembled in Lancaster on the 20th August. The earthquake caused only minor damage.

Swamping the dead and the living. Floods at Crawshaw Booth, north of Rawtenstall, 1895. (LCC/Bacup Library)

1838: A tremendous fall of rain, hailstones and large pieces of ice belted Manchester, Rochdale, Bolton and Preston on the 6th July. Panes of glass in almost every conservatory and factory sky-light were broken and there was much injury to crops.

Flood waters pounded the Victoria Bridge in Manchester on the 16th October, dislodging parts of the central arch. A contractor engaged in repairing the structure suffered a broken leg.

1839: In January, violent storms left a trail of devastation across the county. Winds tore roofs from three of Blackpool's principal hotels – Dickson's, Nickson's and the Yorkshire House, and hundreds of exhausted seabirds were cast up on the shore. Off the Lancashire coast over 20 ships sank or capsized. One of these, the *Crusader*, a Liverpool-Bombay vessel, was besieged by plunderers who stripped her of a valuable cargo of silks and cottons, secreting their booty in wells, pigsties and orchards. Five local men were found guilty of looting and were committed to the House of Correction in Preston. In Liverpool a cotton warehouse was blown down. Cotton fibres were later found in Yorkshire, some 60 miles distant.

1843: Following an earth tremor in March, Manchester suffered high floods, the swollen waters of the Irwell carrying away a temporary footbridge near the New Bailey in October.

1848: Persistent heavy rains at Darwen caused a private dam to burst, as a consequence of which 13 local inhabitants were drowned.

1850: A hurricane of a destructive nature unknown in England for a generation visited Manchester on the 5th February.

1851: Britain's first official air-pollution inspector, Robert Angus Smith, (he coined the term 'acid rain') set up a network of rain-collecting stations around Manchester. He reported his findings to the British Association for the Advancement of

Science, '. . . all the rain was found to contain sulphuric acid in proportion as it approached the town'.

1854–5: Heavy snowfalls and prodigious drifting blocked the Rochdale road in Rossendale for days on end. At Rockcliffe, opposite Greenhill House, the drifts were so deep that the young bloods of the neighbourhood constructed a two storey ice house, the scene, over a number of weeks, for dozens of children's tea parties. In Bolton, where the thermometer plunged to 26 below freezing on the 2nd January, snow reached windowsill height and the mails were delayed for three days.

1859: The *Royal Charter*, a 2,756-ton auxiliary ship en route from Melbourne to Liverpool, foundered off Angelsey on the 25th October. Hurled by hurricane-force winds, giant waves swept away 458 souls. In her strong room, the ship carried a fortune in Australian gold.

1868–9: A combination of high tides and storm force winds brought destruction to Blackpool. The Central Promenade and the Golden Mile were flooded to a depth of several feet, the North Pier was damaged and the fashionable Manchester and Royal Hotels were waterlogged.

1869: Rochdale was rocked by an earthquake on the 15th March.

1870: On the 9th July 1870 Bacup was completely drowned, the local newspaper commenting, 'The rain descended in torrents, indeed we may fearlessly say that a more copious fall has never before been witnessed in this part of the country, nor can we think it has been exceeded in even tropical latitudes.' So high were the floods that most of the mills in the town had their floors ripped away. 'Bacup was, to use a comprehensive term, completely washed out and gutted.'

A travelling pedlar, one 'Jno' Morris was frightened to death by a thunderstorm in Little Lever, Bolton on the 6th September.

Snow shifters in Central Manchester in the 1890s – possibly at the corner of St Ann's Street and Police Street. (C Makepeace)

1872: St Mary's church at Crumpsall was hit by lightning and destroyed.

Robert Angus Smith published *Air and Rain*. In this visionary volume he wrote, 'When the air has so much acid that two or three grains are found in a gallon of the rainwater, or forty parts in a million, there is no hope for vegetation . . . galvanised iron is useless . . . stone and bricks of buildings crumble.'

1880: For the first time in history, a Test Match was entirely washed out by rain. The downpour at Old Trafford created Manchester's soggy reputation.

Piccadilly, Manchester, circa 1895. (C Makepeace)

Flooded Union Street, Bacup, 1895. (LCC/Bacup Library)

Northern attitudes to atmospheric pollution were summed up by a mayor, 'Smoke is an indication of plenty and work (*applause*) – an indication of prosperous times (*cheers*) that all classes of people are employed (*cheers*). Therefore we are proud of our smoke (*prolonged cheers*).'

1884: On the 9th August a hailstorm smashed dozens of glass houses and broke hundreds of windows along a ¼ mile band of countryside at Cowpe and Newchurch End near Bacup. Some of the monstrously large hailstones were described as 'misshapen lumps of ice.'

1889: At 8.15 pm on the 18th January, a lunar rainbow was visible in Bacup.

1894: Brilliant sunshine was enjoyed in Rochdale on the 9th December. 'The surrounding hills looked magnificent under the white covering of fallen snow.'

1898: Southport was one of the snowiest places in Britain on the 23rd November, recording a fall of over 8 inches.

EARLY TWENTIETH CENTURY

27th February 1903: In Like a Lion

In its vilest moods the weather has often been compared to some crazed animal. The comparisons were well founded at the end of February 1903, when a hurricane of intense strength and ferocity brought death and destruction to the whole of the British Isles.

Lancashire and neighbouring counties were badly mauled. An astonishing mishap along the Furness Railway, on the Leven Viaduct near Ulverston, made national headlines. A steam engine and a number of carriages were bowled over. 'It was a miracle that the whole train was not blown into the sea and the frightful Tay Bridge disaster repeated on a smaller scale', said a survivor. The accident injured 33 passengers and another 33 frightened and bewildered souls went missing in the darkness. All were eventually rescued. Like a courageous ship's captain, the train driver remained with his engine throughout the ordeal.

The first towns to bear the brunt of the westerly hurricane were our coastal resorts. In Morecambe there was widespread damage but also an excited curiosity that not even the fear of injury could suppress. Spectators turned out in their hundreds to witness the arrival of the Dublin ferry. Pummelled by the mountainous seas she limped into harbour, carrying a consignment of livestock. Many of the animals had endured an horrendous buffeting and nine cattle and a large number of pigs were so severely injured that they had to be slaughtered at once. Shortly after the ship docked, the maelstrom carried away a 200 yard long section of the pier extension.

In Blackpool the roaring wind and huge waves combined to send spray cascading over the town. 'Every solitary inhabitant has been living in the pleasing uncertainty of whether his roof is going to stay on,' reported one phlegmatic resident. 'Or whether his chimney pots are not sailing through the air. Brave spectators who tried to see the storm were often tossed over like nine-pins and left spluttering in a couple of feet of salt water . . . But the wind and the water had a salubrious effect. They washed Blackpool specklessly clean.'

Further down the coast in Liverpool all telegraphic communication was lost. Here, as in Morecambe, crowds assembled to see a ship in distress. Congregating on the Landing Stage, thousands of people watched as the sailing ship *Fingal* was blown from her anchorage in the river. She drifted helplessly as the imperilled crew took to the rigging, coming to rest near the Hornby Dock. The sailors were eventually saved by the crew of the New Brighton lifeboat.

Inland, the storm raged with even more serious effect. A boy of eight was killed by flying hoarding timber in Burnley, an iron worker received fatal injuries in Warrington and in Camden Place, Preston the roof of a house caved in, fatally crushing a sleeping woman. In the same town, a hansom cab, whilst turning a corner into London Road, was turned over and the cabman hurled a considerable distance. And damage was so severe at Walton-le-Dale Mill that work had to be discontinued.

1909: Something to be Sneezed at

'Owing to the strong breeze that blows up from the river, the poor quarters of Liverpool, with the exception of court and cellar dwellings, do not suffer from stuffiness as much, perhaps, as those of other towns. The winds, however, bring the disadvantage that the dirt which lies in the imperfectly scavenged streets is quickly dried and blown down the throat and nostrils of the passer-by into the houses.' (Report on the Families of Liverpool Labourers)

28th and 29th October 1927: Deep Depression

A swirling low pressure area centred off Ireland brought storm force winds across the north-west of England. Raging at a spit under 100 mph, the typhoon-strong winds whipped up monumental seas, particularly along the Fylde coast. Flooding, structural damage and personal injury were widespread.

Disaster struck in Fleetwood, where an estimated £200,000 worth of damage was caused. Over 700 telephone lines were brought down in the locality, ferry services across the Wyre were suspended and the marooned pupils of Rossall School had to be rescued by boat. Caught at sea, many of Fleetwood's steam trawlers dashed for the shelter of Ramsey Bay.

Other coastal areas had their own horror stories. In Blackpool the new South Shore promenade was 'hit as if by an earthquake'. Giant waves pulverised huge concrete slabs and left seaside shelters in ruins. Parts of the Pleasure Beach, South Shore Baths and the North Pier were mangled, Bonny Street was left under several feet of water, the Star Inn became an island and a tramcar was blown over in Bispham. In neighbouring Lytham, the Dock Road and Preston Road areas were inundated by 'neck-deep' water and the St Anne's sandhills were flooded. Southport also took a battering, a man was killed by flying debris in Morecambe, and in Liverpool two crewmen of a barge in Sandon Dock were blown into the water and rescued in total darkness.

Inland, the storm led to flooding in Preston, where the Ribble overflowed its banks, Blackburn and district suffered a blitzkrieg

Flaking out . . . as if the Grand National fences weren't hazard enough! (Watercolour by John Beer. City of Liverpool Public Libraries)

of showering slates and masonry and in Bolton several people had to be treated at the infirmary for lacerations and broken limbs. The wind blew in windows at Manchester's City Hall and it toppled a large elm tree, which crashed onto overhead wires, disrupting tram services.

Weather Notes 1900 – 1930

1902: The Russian barquentine *Matador* from Riga was caught in a storm off Crosby. Driven ashore by the ferocious wind she broke her back and was a total loss.

1908: During an exceptionally cold winter, Bolton recorded a low of −13.9°F.

1909: Heaven watchers all over the North of England enjoyed a brilliant display of the Northern Lights on the evening of the 25th September.

1911: Manchester sweltered in a temperature of 81.3°F on the 11th July. A man died of heat exhaustion in the Eagle Mills premises of Joseph Crook and Co. Ltd in Bolton.

1912: The name of Stonyhurst entered the history books after the locality recorded 38 'thunder days' during the year.

1914: Referring to the plight of haymakers on Pennine farms during a Lords debate on atmospheric pollution, one speaker said, '. . . they often emerge from their labours in the condition of colliers . . .'

In the shade . . . a member of the 'Hole in the Wall' gang? Liverpool, 1904. (City of Liverpool Public Libraries)

Central Manchester, March 1923. (C Makepeace)

1915: Long johns sales soared after a winter low of −13.3°F was recorded in Morecambe.

1916–17: Known as the Soldiers' Winter, this was the fourth coldest on record. On All Fools' Day, the temperature in Burnley fell to −12°F.

1919: Snow fell on the Pennines on the 20th September.

1920: The swollen river Brock, a tributary of the Wyre, washed away a bridge on the A6 and halted traffic. A railway viaduct was also damaged and the banks of the river were torn away at New Bridge.

1921: In April, thousands of star-gazers lined the Promenade and Princess Parade in Blackpool to witness a partial eclipse of the sun.

1924: On the 21st of September, 85 mph gales did great damage in Blackpool.

1926: Whipped up by a raging March wind, a storm sandblasted Blackpool.

1927: A violent wind storm and high tides brought severe flooding to the port of Fleetwood on the 28th October. The gale – recorded at 96 mph in Southport – brought widespread disruption to electricity supplies. Sea spray was carried several miles inland, leading to the formation of salt crystals on power line insulators.

1928: Bank holiday crowds on the 29th August trained their binoculars on a waterspout spiralling above the sea off Blackpool.

THE WEATHER IN
THE THIRTIES

A Miscellany

1931: Flooding caused over £2,000 worth of damage to the Rawtenstall Electricity Works at Hareholme, putting 22 mills in Rawtenstall and Bacup out of action.

1933: Freezing conditions throughout the county during January exacerbated the plight of the unemployed.

On the 20th June, a hail and lightning storm swept across Merseyside. Flood waters which were over 10 ft deep in Bootle swept a cyclist to his death.

1935: On the 16th May, one foot of snow fell on the high ground above Blackburn.

A northerly airstream brought continuous snowfalls to Lancashire on the 19th May. In West Kirby the white stuff fell without let up for 5½ hours, giving a covering of 2 inches. Temperatures remained just below freezing throughout the day.

Twice during the exceptionally wet month of September (according to the old maxim, 'September either dries up rivers or sweeps away bridges') Bacup was swamped. Over a period of two days the river Irwell twice broke its banks, causing massive

Spring 1937 – A snow drop somewhere on the 'tops'. (Mr T Lyons)

damage and destruction. The rain washed hundreds of tons of soil onto the railway line at Shawforth and the Stacksteads recreation ground became a miniature lake. Housewives in Plantation Street and Market Street were hard pressed to combat the ingress of water rushing off the hillsides. The torrents ripped away rooftops and poured through ceilings, completely devastating many homes.

1936: Dense mist was blamed for two airport fatalities in Blackpool where the Isle of Man flight struck a hangar, killing the pilot and one female passenger.

In November, Manchester suffered treacle-thick fog for 10 days, '. . . a loathsome black slime coated everything.'

1938: Manchester once again had the dubious distinction of hosting an entirely washed out Test Match at Old Trafford . . . all those limp cucumber sandwiches!

The rain gauge in Bacup recorded an all-time monthly high for October of 14.64 inches.

A foggy day in Manchester. A photograph taken at 12 noon on 12th February 1934 in Piccadilly. (C Makepeace)

1939: In many places in the county, Christmas was the coldest since 1894. Manchester recorded 33° of frost and long stretches of the Mersey were covered in ice. The cold weather brought a harvest for plumbers, much of the trouble being attributed to the fact that the majority of houses were unoccupied for lengthy periods. On his return home from work, one Manchester resident found his front door jammed solid with an accumulation of ice.

THE WEATHER IN
THE FORTIES

January 1940: Smog in Manchester

So vile was the poisonous cloud that enveloped Manchester during the first January of the war, that some sufferers blamed the Germans. For four days the noxious mixture of fog and pollutants choked the city, causing widespread respiratory problems and coating everything in a tacky bloom. Drifting in through hastily slammed doors, the gas soiled laundry and badly affected commercial establishments, contaminating all uncovered food products, discolouring window displays and tarnishing furniture and jewellery. 'It was thick and brown and could be smelt and tasted,' said a King Street bookseller. 'It was as though some impish person had blown a filthy, sticky, evil-smelling film over everything. It looked like dust, but when touched it felt greasy and adhesive.' Coupled with exceptionally low temperatures, the smog led to a marked increase in the death rate.

29th January 1940: Keep the Home Fires Burning

For the first time in history, a Scottish express train was held up by drifted snow south of Preston. Large areas of Lancashire and the north were completely cut off, the War Office announcing an immediate postponement of leave for British Expeditionary

How deep is my valley? Cross Stone Road, above the Vicarage, Todmorden, January 1940. (Mrs M Brierley)

Force personnel 'owing to the intensely severe weather conditions.'

The 400 passengers aboard the LMS train near Preston were cheered by assistance from the local council. Hot meals were provided and Preston Public Baths was placed at their disposal.

With no buses or trains running in Blackburn, conditions were described as the worst on record and many villages in the Chorley district were 'unapproachable'. Manchester was almost isolated and hundreds of soldiers on weekend leave were unable to return to their training quarters. For the first time in 40 years, Southport was without an electric train service to Liverpool and Crossens.

Walking on water. The river Ribble near the main line railway bridge, Preston, January 1940. (Lancashire County Library)

30th January 1940: 'Delayed Action Weather'

'The novel wartime device of permitting no weather for printing purposes except that which is a fortnight old is not without its merits. It may not baffle the Germans, but it does produce a gush of stimulating details when the pressure is suddenly released and the news floods forth like the water from a burst pipe . . . It is no longer a mystery why so many domestic boilers took it into their heads to explode in so many different parts of the country during the first half of this month. It has ceased to be a matter of conjecture why so many of the younger sort "fell into" ponds, streams and canals during the same period . . . and why an unfortunate lady of Islington was found sitting in a solid block of ice in her bath . . . Once we should have known about such things in a mere day-to-day trickle; now they reach us in one grand spectacular burst when the fourteen days' thaw sets in at the Ministry of Information . . .' (*Manchester Guardian*)

8th April 1943: Air Raid

Whilst the 8th Army was pursuing Rommel in North Africa, weather news back home got short shrift. Destructive gales in Manchester were hardly mentioned in the *Evening Chronicle*, despite scores of toppled chimneys and at least one fatality. Tragically, dislodged masonry smashed the glass roof of a laundry at the Home Office School for Girls in Northenden Road, killing one of the pupils.

1946–7: Arctic Lancashire

The winter of 1946–7 ranks alongside that of 1963 as one of the harshest weather events of the 20th century. In the aftermath of a debilitating war, unprepared Britain was brought to its knees, suffering successive blizzards whose malevolence drew grim parallels with the frequent attacks of the Luftwaffe. The freezing temperatures brought almost total paralysis. Freight trains were frozen to the lines and passenger services were severely disrupted. Roads were persistently blocked, rivers became ribbons of ice and, in some places, the sea froze over. Combined with food shortages (bread was rationed following a poor harvest), absenteeism, strikes, short-time working and a lethal paucity of coal, gas and electricity, the weather brought misery and death, desperate families burning furniture and even books and shoes in an attempt to keep warm. But, as they had stiffened the labial sinews during the war, so they responded to another of the Prime Minister's radio calls for economies, by eating less, by sharing baths and going to bed early, and by being ever ready with shovels and spades for the daily contests with the snow.

January 1940. Bottom of Cross Stone Road, Todmorden. (Mrs M Brierley)

The first snowfall of the winter swept across Lancashire on the 3rd December and, with brief and cruelly deceptive interludes of fine weather, it continued to snow, the temperature sometimes not rising above freezing point night or day for weeks on end. Between the 22nd January and the 17th March, snow fell every single day somewhere in Great Britain, making this winter the snowiest on record.

The pre-Christmas snowflakes – ominously the biggest in living memory – were succeeded by hard frosts, the harsh conditions retarding work on scores of north-west building sites. The erection of 200 desperately needed pre-fabricated concrete houses for the Salford Corporation was put back by weeks. The approaching festive season brought only a little cheer. Electricity and gas supplies were cut by up to 50% and frost and fog bound roads threatened a consignment of 25,000 Argentinian turkeys despatched from Liverpool to Manchester.

The new year started badly across the county, coal shortages closing a number of mills in Bacup, Bury and Burnley. On the 6th January snowploughs were out in Blackburn, and Liverpool suffered the worst power cut of the winter. Two days later, convoys of trucks, driven by ex-army personnel, delivered vital supplies to north-west towns. On that same day a thaw set in, the *Liverpool Echo* supporting the much cursed weather experts with an article headlined 'Don't Always Blame The Weather Clerk'. It claimed, 'British meteorologists have an astonishing record of accuracy to their credit.' With impeccable timing the accompanying forecast predicted 'considerably milder than of late,' and on the 9th January the sun peeped through . . . briefly.

For a few days, Lancashire weather became less newsworthy, although reports from abroad continued to fill the pages, the plight of the people of Hamburg, 16 of whom froze to death, being reported in the *Manchester Guardian*. Frost bite afflicted thousands of homeless Germans and local gaols were full of prisoners arrested for stealing coal and food.

Back home, the blizzards arrived in earnest during the second half of January. Predictably, the snowflakes were predominantly white ... except in Bootle where 'it snowed soot'. An extensive area of the borough, centred on Hawthorne Road and Aintree Road, was covered in a black mantle overnight, householders first becoming aware of the problem when cats returned home for breakfast, 'sooty paw marks leading to an investigation.'

More conventionally, Liverpudlians woke up to a dusting of snow on the 26th January. It was only three-tenths of an inch deep. Elsewhere in the county the drifts were measured in yards. The news of Al Capone's death on the 27th January lifted spirits for a while, but by the 29th temperatures had nose-dived and fuel shortages caused short-time working in Bolton cotton mills, the *Manchester Evening Chronicle* adding its own gobbet of mirth, trumpeting 'Antarctica Is Warmer.' The newspaper went on to describe the late arrival of the *Mancunian* in Kings Cross, noting, 'One good effect of the snow and cold was to keep motor-cars out of London. At ten this morning in Piccadilly one could count the cars between the Ritz and the Circus ...'

As the weather worsened, and as precious coal supplies were eked out, one minuscule Lancashire industry thrived, the Dutch proprietor of the 250 acres of peat fields at Astley Moss, near Worsley, working round the clock to meet demand.

The month ended with the biggest electricity cuts ever made in Britain. Large parts of the Manchester suburbs were plunged into darkness for several hours. Gas pressure reductions added to the gloom and in Liverpool on the 30th January a 44 inch water main was cracked by the frost, sending a miniature tidal wave surging into 100 houses near Old Swan and flooding parts of Knotty Ash Station. Some 24 hours later there was more drama when the Hallé Orchestra arrived back in Manchester after a snowy adventure on the moor top between Ripponden and Denshaw. Returning from a concert in Halifax, their coach foundered in deep drifts and the musicians had to dig with their bare hands to extricate the vehicle. Guest conductor Nicolai Malko, a former resident of Murmansk, expressed the view that his experience would not have been surpassed in Arctic Russia.

Doom-laden skies brought yet more snow. Then absolute disaster! On an icy Highbury pitch on the 1st February, Manchester United slipped to an ignominious 6–2 defeat at the feet of Arsenal, and not even a humorous press report from Paris could raise an Old Trafford titter. Fans were po-faced at the news that a Gallic duel was cancelled 'because it was too cold.' The contributing journalist obviously supported Liverpool, penning a four-verse poem celebrating the non-event. You will catch the drift from the following extract:

'Fields of honour, chill and ghastly,
Fill my chastened soul with dread;
I regard myself as vastly better off tucked up in bed.
Thus forsaking all my former plans for someone's swift
  decease,
Till the world is somewhat warmer,
I pursue the path of peace.'

There was little else to raise a smile. On the 4th and 5th February, blizzards again ravaged communications. A chilly group of 25 passengers was marooned overnight when an engine ground to a halt in a gully between Royton Junction and Shaw on the Manchester to Rochdale line. Oldham had its heaviest snowfall for many years and drifts up to 20 ft deep cut off scores of villages and blocked dozens of other railway lines. In the Nelson area, all roads to Roughlee and Barley were closed. Throughout Lancashire thousands of workers, assisted by troops and German prisoners, dug for victory over the remorseless weather, battling day by day with shovels to reopen vital routes. It was a time of great hardship but also a time of exceptional fortitude, heroism and friendship. Neighbourliness had its finest hour! Communities organised communal games and whist drives, they shared dwindling supplies of potatoes and flour, and home cooking and baking reached new heights of improvisation and ingenuity. Imagine housewives today making nutritious meals from a pig's head! And, despite the appalling conditions, people kept working. Given the option of shivering at work or returning home, 3,000 operatives at Roe's aircraft factory at Chadderton put on pullovers. One worker from the Fairey Aviation Works at Stockport remembers trudging home along snowbound roads, treading on the roofs of buried cars. Several Bacup miners recall walking 2 miles on wall tops to get to their pit. When pay day arrived they discovered that they had been docked time for clocking on late.

February wore on, affecting everything from the mundane to the mercurial. Glass bottle production in St Helens was dramatically slowed and, with scores of cotton mills closed for want of fuel, over 57,000 workers were made idle. Some enterprising concerns kept going, the manager at Bolton Leathers Ltd buying up an army dump of old rubber and surplus cartridge cases to keep his boilers burning. With arable crops buried under ice fields, only meagre supplies of vegetables reached the shops and there were long queues at greengrocers, and such were the appalling conditions at sea that fish landings were meagre, the shortage of cod and haddock threatening the chip shop trade. All in all, those impish weather gods really had cause for merriment during that vile month. In Manchester Road, Bolton, on the 9th, firemen doused a burning building and slipped like demented skaters as the hose water froze, and, across in Liverpool, Sir Adrian Boult and the overcoated members of the Liverpool Philharmonic had to rehearse in a theatre foyer following a power cut in the concert hall.

By February the 10th industry was almost at a standstill and over one million workers across the region were idle as a consequence of electricity cuts and coal shortages. Throughout the Lancashire conurbation, thousands of confused workers from Ferranti, Metropolitan Vickers, Mather and Platt and other major firms roamed the streets in utter confusion. It was time for action.

Councillors debated the crisis by candlelight in Salford and, in the House of Commons, Mr Winston Churchill rose to his feet and boomed, 'If of course the anger of the country at the ordeals to which it is being subjected should result in the expulsion from power of our present rulers, it would indeed be a merciful deliverance' (*Opposition cheers*).

Big guns, both political and incendiary, were wheeled out in a determined attempt to beat the elements. On the 15th February a flame thrower was used in a vain attempt to thaw out the blocked railway line near Royton Junction. And then a meteorological practical joke. 'Ray of Hope', announced one evening newspaper, noting, 'Hope sprang anew in many an icy breast when a distinguished stranger looked in on Manchester this afternoon. It was the sun.' But a warning came from the 'Met' office, curbing the early exuberance. 'Don't let it fool you. The temperature is still 1 degree below freezing point, and the thaw will be very slight and very temporary. Tonight's temperature will be well below freezing point. Sorry folks!'

True to the predictions, the blizzards returned with renewed ferocity. The river Sept froze over in New Mills and many more mills joined the rash of closures, a Cotton Spinners Association representative calculating lost production at 50 million yards of cloth. Conditions for Lancashire farmers were truly horrendous but even here there was nothing to compare with the experiences of a stock breeder in Market Rasen, Lincolnshire, where three sheep were pecked to death by ravenous crows.

The night of the 23rd February was one of the coldest nights of the winter. Burnley recorded 30° of frost and, in neighbouring Cheshire, the river Dee froze in Chester. Three days later, borne on a 40 mph wind, a fresh blizzard brought new chaos. All sailings from Liverpool were cancelled, many unfortunate vessels still at sea were hurled ashore and more roads and railway lines were blocked.

All hands to the pump. Clearing mud after floods in Broughton, 1946.
(Manchester Public Libraries/Solo)

February calendars were torn up in disgust, the advent of March bringing hopes of better weather. Throughout the county on the 3rd, thousands of employees returned to work, long queues forming at factory gates despite the lack of heating. 'It almost looked as if someone was selling nylons,' reported one observer. Everyone waited for the great thaw to begin. Millions were disappointed as the nightmarish blizzards returned on the 6th.

'Manchester Express Lost Somewhere In Snow' read one stark headline. Railway timetables across the country were cut to ribbons and hundreds of roads disappeared under the heaviest snowfalls of the winter. Once more unto the breach came armies of snow shifters. Hundreds of troops and prisoners of war toiled to clear railway lines at Woodhead and Hadfield and in the Rossendale Valley, where every road was impassable, women and boys joined the gangs of workmen in the long dig. Some villagers hereabouts had been isolated for weeks on end. One woman lamented, 'No lorries have been able to pass through the local roads for 5 weeks. My kitchen has been so cold even with a small fire that the snow brought into the house has frozen on the kitchen floor. Even the water in the mop bucket froze. The snow has been so high that it covered the first floor windows. We have had to burn hen coops to make a little fire for the children.'

The long awaited melt-down started on the 10th March, and with it came the floods. Catastrophe struck Selby and district in Yorkshire. Here in Lancashire there were only minor problems, although, as a precaution, Salford residents moved furniture upstairs after the Irwell rose nearly 4 ft.

Spring arrived and farmers raced to sow their crops, working through the night with the use of headlights. It was a time for reflection and some recrimination. On the 19th March Mr P. Noel-Baker, Secretary of State for Air, was asked to supply an explanation in the House of Commons about 'the incorrect weather forecasts given by his department during the recent cold spell.' 'To my regret,' he replied, 'I must admit that the science of meteorology still leaves much to be desired' (*laughter and cheers*).

Snippets from the Roaring Forties

1940: The winter of 1939–40 was the third coldest in the region this century. Some blue-toed Lancastrians wore layers of rags and cast-offs in an attempt to keep warm . . . but the *Manchester Guardian* attempted to keep up appearances. At the end of January the newspaper published an article about winter fashion, showing a photograph of a debonair young lady in a 'Molyneux brown and beige tweed coat trimmed with beaver'. The correspondent wrote, 'Warm clothes offer opportunities for style; and it is only in winters such as the present that style and need really join hands and become obvious...people are hugging their furs and their thickest tweeds, supported in the utilitarian direction by the militarisation of the nation. Military coats, or rather coats with a military atmosphere are persisting into spring...'

Manchester, Salford and the surrounding areas were heavily bombed by the Luftwaffe on the nights of the 22nd and 23rd December. The resultant fires were brought under control but, on Christmas Eve, strong north-easterly winds fanned the embers, causing further severe fire damage to property.

1941: Guided by bright moonlight on the 2nd May, almost 100 German bombers targeted Liverpool and Bootle.

1943: Gales were clocked in Manchester on the 7th April at 90 mph.

After a week of very high temperatures, the hot spell came to a dousing end on the 31st July. In Wigan, a 100 ft high dust cloud whipped up by strong winds, preceded a storm of heavy rain. In West Kirby, 1.02 inches of rain fell in just 16 minutes.

1944: Leyland was pelted with 1.2 inches of hail on the 30th June.

During November, Rochdale endured almost perpetual rain. The recorded 8.1 inches was the highest for 10 years.

1945: On the 25th and 26th January, Morecambe experienced its coldest night since records began in 1896, the temperature dropping to −13°F.

In April, weathering and the effects of seepage were implicated in a bizarre railway accident in Abram, near Wigan. A speeding steam engine and 13 loaded wagons plunged down a yawning chasm after the plugging on an old mine shaft suddenly collapsed.

1947: A 75 mph gale brought down a 120 ft high stone and brick chimney at New Mills on the 16th March. The catastrophic crash during the early hours went unheard!

In August, following a long summer drought, fell fires swept across Wyresdale. Consuming the tinder-dry heather, the blaze resisted the combined efforts of Lancashire fire brigades and raged for days unchecked. Moorland sheep and birds suffered badly. Land near Tarnbrook, formerly used as a gunnery range, erupted violently as unexploded shells were detonated by the flames. During the month Blackpool enjoyed average temperatures of 75°F.

1948: Between the 22nd November and the 1st December, dense fog choked most of Europe. It extended from the Thames estuary to the Welsh borders, northwards to Yorkshire and Lancashire and across a 1,200 mile belt of Finland. All shipping stopped, the Berlin Airlift was halted and in the near blind conditions there were several train crashes.

Eyes down! Shovelling near Rob's Grave, Thornley, January 1940.
(Norwyn Photos, Preston)

THE WEATHER IN
THE FIFTIES

9th March 1955: Blasted Weather

Drastic measures were required to dislodge a 20 ft high overhanging cornice of snow threatening the Manchester to Sheffield road at the Snake Pass, highway maintenance reaching explosive heights as 10 gelignite charges were buried deep in the white carpet. Fears of an avalanche closed the road as, for the first time on record, a demolition expert pushed the plunger blasting thousands of tons of ice skyward. 'I am quite pleased with the result', said the engineer in charge. 'It exceeded my expectations.'

April 1957: Spanish Highs

Bound for an English airport, an aeroplane carried a secret weapon. Stowed alongside the team boots was an anticyclone... a concentrated load of high pressure...target Manchester!

The pride of Spanish football, Real Madrid, arrived at Old Trafford in brilliant sunshine and for the three days that the players were in town they enjoyed uninterrupted blue skies, the unfortunate Manchester United groundsman having to soak the hallowed pitch himself with water drawn from Haweswater in the Lake District, some 80 miles distant.

Now you see it; now you don't. Turn to next page! Above the Moorcock Inn, Blackstone Edge, looking towards Littleborough, 1957. (G Stott)

Keeping the legend of Manchester rainfall alive, the pre-match press comments had referred to our typically English weather. 'Soaked turf and cool conditions suit our lads best', boasted one journalist as the temperature rose into the 60s. Ditching his gaberdine, Terence F. Usher, Information Officer to the City of Manchester, was quick to spot the opportunity of beating the Costa Del Sol at its own game. 'On Wednesday we had over 13 hours sunshine,' he beamed. 'Manchester has, in fact, one of the nicest autumn, winter and spring climates in Britain, with a high mean temperature and little rain.' The Real Madrid players were really impressed, answering the two goals from Tommy Taylor and Bobby Charlton with two pearlers of their own. The springtime tonic did them a power of good. They eventually beat United 3–5 on aggregate and went on to lift the European Cup.

1958 – 1966: 'Road's Blocked John'

If campaign medals were struck to reward dedication in the winter field, our snow clearing crews would sport chestfuls, the gritters alone maintaining vital road links, often working round the clock in arctic conditions. Typical of this hardworking and largely unsung body of men is retired foreman J.C. Clarke of Rishton near Blackburn. He writes of his experiences working for Rishton Council between 1958 and 1966, 'I was the only driver, so I had to go out at night, many times all night as the roads were snow bound and exceptionally deep on the top roads around Wilpshire and Ribchester. The method of gritting the roads – as we had no machines – was a wagon with three men on the back, one either side and one over the rear. Each one had a shovel and a stick which was used to flick the salt. The speed was about 4 miles per hour. Some roads were very bad. We had to dig through as some people were trapped in their homes and we had to dig cars out sometimes as the snowplough was no use in 10 feet drifts. I used to go to bed very early – 8 pm – to try and get a few hours sleep before the police came to say, "road's blocked John".'

John Clarke and crew, snow shifting around Rishton, 1958. (Mr J Clarke)

21st August 1959: Merseyside Monsoon

'Cloudbursts, torrential rain, blitz-like thunderclaps and violent lightning flashes brought storm chaos to Britain yesterday', declared a *Liverpool Daily Post* reporter, reviewing the events of a quite extraordinary day. Hit by a double weather whammy at 5 pm and then again at 8.30 pm, Liverpool was swamped by driving curtains of rain, so dense that, at times, the sides of many city streets were invisible from the opposite pavements.

The evening rush hour was stopped in its tracks. Houses and commercial premises were flooded, manhole covers popped like corks and roadways and railway lines were ripped up. 'The storm was so great', said a Corporation official, 'that the drains filled within minutes. They just couldn't stand up to it. We've had floods before but nothing like this.'

City centre stores and nearby homes were inundated. In Rachel Street, off Scotland Road, men in bathing costumes swam to the rescue of beleaguered pensioners. Bold Street was described as a river in full spate and in Great Nelson Street the water reached windowsill height. Customers in the Kardomah Café in Church Street ran to safety as water trickled around their feet and in the grocery department of the Liverpool Cooperative in Byron Street a recently delivered consignment of tea and coffee was ruined. In the same store, all kinds of goods were found floating in the chandlery section. Damage across the city ran into many thousands of pounds.

Fifties File

1950: Severe gales dimmed the Blackpool Lights and electricians were out in force to repair the damage.

1952: Borne on the wind, '. . . the smoke carried far into the country districts of the Pennines coated the needles of conifers so

76

thickly that it must have restricted photosynthesis...' (Forestry Commission)

1953: Sympathies were extended to seaside families along the east coast following one of the worst peacetime disasters in British history. On the 31st January, fierce storms killed some 300 people.

Snow fell over the highest parts of Lancashire on the 3rd June as Queen Elizabeth II was being crowned in Westminster Abbey.

In the last week of June, thunderstorms over east Lancashire churned up industrial waste in the Calder and its tributaries, polluting the Ribble. Thousands of fish died along an 18 mile stretch of the river from Hacking Boat near Ribchester to Preston.

1954: Several Lancashire children fell through thin ice and drowned during January. The 20th of the month was the wettest in Preston since 1876. In total, 2.21 inches or 29,666,070 gallons of rain fell in the borough in the 24 hour period.

1955: Normally snow-free Blackpool woke up to a 5 ft deep mantle on the 19th January.

1957: One of the most powerful earthquakes ever recorded in England sent shock waves across eleven English counties on the 11th February. Distinct tremors were felt in Blackpool.

THE WEATHER IN
THE SIXTIES

4th December 1962: Fog Blind

'A city groping about in nil visibility', declared a London newspaper as a blanket of fog descended over England, affecting 125,000 miles of road. In the capital, the lethal cocktail of fog, soot, sulphur and other pollutants caused at least 32 deaths, 6 people actually dropping dead in the street.

Driving conditions were treacherous across Lancashire, where traffic was reduced to a crawl. A van driver was killed in a five car collision on the A6 in Bolton and a second tragedy occurred on the towpath of the Rochdale Canal at Failsworth. Here a disorientated 45 year old woman fell into the water and drowned.

All flights were grounded at Manchester Airport and the fog was so thick along the coast that a trawler returning from a trip to Iceland was stranded just 50 yards from Fleetwood promenade.

1963: Iceberg Island

'Often pure white. Spotless, innocent to behold. Picturesque and powerfully impressive. But primed with lurking dangers. Silently sinister. A white spectre, tightening its grip and clawing out at the life-blood of a nation.'

Foggy day in Preston town. One householder in a Preston smokeless zone, faced with greatly increased bills for the special fuel required, described the position as farcical 'since locomotives at Preston railway station, less than a quarter of a mile from my home, continue to be the chief source of muck'. (Lancashire Evening Post)

This was but one of scores of highly descriptive passages from local newspapers recalling the notorious winter of 1963. Nationally, the weather conditions left at least 49 people dead. Internationally, the below zero temperatures led to the river Danube freezing over for the first time in memory, to the Neptune fountain in Florence freezing rock solid and to hunger-crazed wolves in central Greece attacking villagers. The coldest winter on record in Manchester and many other parts of this county, that exceptional season of 1963, lasting 77 days, has gone down in history as the cruelest this century.

It began happily enough. The pre-Christmas flurries of snow evoked the dreams of Bing Crosby and as the thermometer plummeted to 18 degrees of frost on the 23rd December one Blackburn pensioner rejoiced at the cold, having received an early seasonal charitable gift of a hot-water bottle. 'I've always wanted one', she beamed.

As the old year ended, after smashing surface ice with pick-axes, 16 supposedly sane men were gripped by a communal lunacy, plunging into the frigid depths of Lee Dam at Mankinholes to raise money for a new baths. There was less to smile about on the 1st January when 80 mph winds ushered in a raw cold. In Burnley, operatives at the Belling factory were sent home as it was too cold to work. By the 3rd January, five Saddleworth villages were marooned by deep drifts and the whole of Britain was ravaged by blizzards, one leader writer referring to the nation as 'Iceberg Island'.

All forms of transportation were made perilous. Wheeled vehicles were smothered by snow and there was a run on salt in Blackburn and elsewhere. Apart from skating and tobogganing, sport was virtually wiped out. Most league football games were cancelled – on the 9th January the *Manchester Guardian* published a photograph showing the England and Blackpool captain Jimmy Armfield skating on the Bloomfield Road ground – and even four legs proved little guarantee of traction, the Holcombe Harriers Hunt calling off their meeting 'because no self respecting fox would leave his den.'

A series of blinding snow storms in mid-January brought 'white out' conditions, particularly to rural areas. Canals froze up and so bad were the incessant frosts that Darwen sewage works was nearly forced to shut down. Frozen gas pipes led to a rash of domestic poisonings – there were fatalities in Church and Nelson – and in myriad Lancashire homes there was the heartbreak of burst water pipes, 1,000 properties in Blackburn alone being inundated. Freezing water did have its

Blocked in Burnley, January 1963. (Lancashire Evening Telegraph)

compensations. On the 19th January, skaters were out on Windermere for the first time since 1947.

The 20th January was a black day. Two climbers were swept to their deaths in the Chew Valley at Greenfield, near Oldham, an avalanche carrying their bodies 200 ft, and at Belthorn near Blackburn, after abandoning his car, a company director battled his way home in a snowstorm, perishing only ½ mile from safety. It could have been worse. Leaving Wycoller Hall, near Colne, in a blizzard, eight scouts were rescued, having spent the night huddled up in a van, singing songs to keep up their spirits.

The arctic noose tightened, vulnerable old folk suffering badly. On the 21st January, the Mayor of Blackburn launched an

Sprinting for the No. 4 in Lord Street, Southport, 1963. (LCC/Bacup Library)

emergency 'Food Flying Squad' to get vital fuel and foodstuffs to 2,000 pensioners. Then temperatures dropped even lower. The worst series of gas main fractures for over 30 years interrupted supplies and two elderly men were asphyxiated in Burnley. Bone cracking frosts caused large patches of thin ice to form on the Mersey and there were unprecedented demands for sticks, crutches and plaster of Paris! The cancellation of all sport had an unusual effect in Bolton. More books were issued at the Central Library on the 21st than at any time in its 110 year history, and, as the meteorologists argued about their air streams and anticyclones, one gentleman wrote to a Manchester newspaper, registering his own theories on the causes of the bad weather:

A no flow area – Southport Pier, 1963. (LCC/Bacup Library)

'Sir – It will not have escaped the notice of your more percipient readers that this present Arctic spell follows the arbitrary adoption of degrees centigrade by the weathermen. Things were rarely as bad when we were on the old Fahrenheit scale.
Yours faithfully
J.M. Winterbottom'

On the 22nd January, 50,000 consumers in Manchester suffered burst or frozen pipes and, at the Clayton Secondary School in the city, striking pupils lobbied the education offices about the chilly conditions in class. The month ended with East Lancashire losing over 5 million gallons of water per day through frost-fractured pipes. Liverpool lost 8 million gallons and in the Ribble valley water supplies were delivered by beer tanker. Across the

North Sea there was a grim prediction, West German experts suggesting that if the conditions continued the entire Baltic Sea might freeze up.

February brought comparisons with the winter of 1895 as fresh blizzards swept in, 'cutting Britain in two'. The Oldham and Saddleworth districts were isolated by mountainous heaps of snow, Belthorn and Tockholes were cut off again and, on the 7th, two heavy locomotives fitted with snowploughs rammed a drift on the railway line at Thornton-in-Craven, tearing up the rails as they came to grief. A huge steam crane came to the rescue and also foundered. Those people who remembered the long winter of 1947 dreaded the coming weeks, but slowly the temperatures rose and by the middle of the month the memorable winter of 1963 came to a close.

18th July 1964: Horror in the Raindrops

The dramatic headline in the *Lancashire Evening Telegraph* souvenir edition of July 25th 1964 heralded an 18 page account of devastation on a massive scale, millions of gallons of 'fat raindrops that hit the pavements and bounced a foot off the ground' combining to disrupt transport, inundate factories, mills and houses and wash away dozens of homes across East Lancashire.

The county was in holiday mood, Manchester weathermen predicting weekend sunshine with temperatures in the 70s. Typically, though, Saturday was Pak-a-Mac weather, heavy rain bringing flooding to Bacup. Near Darwen, lightning hit an overhead cable, sparking a mill fire at Brocklehead Farm, Eccleshill. Undeterred, thousands of families boarded buses and trains, intent on a precious fortnight by the sea. But around lunchtime the black clouds gathered, a deadly cocktail of rain, hail and lightning bringing misery and terror, delivered by two consecutive storms.

Getting sloshed. Outside the New Inn, Todmorden, 1966. (Mrs M Brierley)

Emergency telephone lines were jammed with frantic requests for help as torrents of water poured from the hillsides, ripping up roads and railway lines, demolishing walls and houses and erupting, geyser-like, from overloaded sewers. Statistics toppled before the onrush of water. On that extraordinary day, Burnley was pelted with golf ball size hailstones and 1.22 inches of rain fell – the highest 24 hour total in living memory – and at Mitchell's Reservoir, above the ill-fated Rising Bridge, a tropical total of 3.1 inches was recorded. Poor Haslingden was hit harder than any other town in the area, trees, soil, masonry, other debris and a 6 inch mantle of hailstones blocking culverts, sending rivers raging through the streets, where the flood claimed its first tragic victim. Pensioner Mrs Emma Donald was drowned

'I'll plop round this afternoon.' South Promenade, Blackpool, 1967. (Blackpool Gazette & Herald)

before she could open her door. A few miles south-west, a number of landslides blocked railway lines. Water cascaded down the steep moorland slopes above the Sough Tunnel on the Blackburn–Manchester line between Darwen and Bromley Cross,

'And I've just put on fresh nylons.' Lancashire County Fire Brigade in action in Blackburn Road, Darwen, July 1964. *(Lancashire Evening Telegraph)*

closing both entrances with hundreds of tons of earth and rock. Nearby, the river Darwen was in spate, rampaging down its valley, towards Blackburn, with tremendous speed. A 5 ft high tidal wave carried away the parapet of the Hollin Street bridge, allowing water to pour unchecked into 236 Blackburn homes. Elsewhere it was the same soggy tale, the residents of Padiham, Colne, Barley and Accrington all having their own horror stories. Memories of events at Rising Bridge are the stuff of nightmares.

The air 'thickened and thickened until it became pregnant with a million volts of terror', reported the *Evening Telegraph*, a few graphic sentences describing the awesome 'whiplash from the skies'. Floodwater rushed through the village at a vast rate of knots, carrying away two houses and a garage. Mr Sid Hatton described the loss of his home, 'The river off the moors flows under our house. We could always hear it when it was shallow. But on Saturday it roared. I heard my place creaking and decided to get out quick. I'd just got through the door and was wading thigh deep in water when everything went down.'

Throughout their ordeal, the people of East Lancashire displayed considerable fortitude and selflessness. A twister at Calder Vale Mill, Barrowford, 17 year old Jean Byker, was hailed as a heroine by elderly residents of Duckworth Street. Hitching up her skirt, she ferried hot tea and sandwiches, using a ladder to reach pensioners trapped in upstairs rooms. Magnificent work was also done by the emergency services and by volunteers, some of whom broke off their holidays to assist with rescues and the heart-rending work of mopping up. There were isolated incidents of looting but, overall, 'Lancashire neighbourliness had one of its finest hours. People grinned and bore it and even had time to laugh at themselves; at respectable mothers covered from head to foot in slime; at dads who did the cooking while their wives washed filthy clothes and at the children who were playing amid the flotsam and jetsam of sopping armchairs and mud-coloured axminsters which transformed whole streets into rubbish dumps.'

In the cold light of analysis, the experts gave their verdicts, drainage specialist Mr G.T. Jury, Borough Surveyor of Haslingden commenting, 'I have travelled all over the world and have never seen anything like it before. Not even a tropical monsoon could compare with Saturday's downpour.' 'By the law of averages,' assured one sober weatherman, 'Lancashire should last have had a storm like this in 1784. The next catastrophe could be in the year 2144.'

14th July 1967: Flash, Bang, Wallop

What a picture the weather made that balmy summer night! In the skies above Merseyside around 3 am, booming thunder and

Don't drop the baby. Floods in Princess Street, Blackburn, July 1964. (Lancashire Evening Telegraph)

forked lightning played an effulgent duet in one of the most violent electrical storms on record. Many sleepers were catapulted from their beds and they rushed to bedroom windows to enjoy the spectacle. The storm had rolled in, following a hot and humid day during which the temperature had reached 78.5°F.

Accompanied by lashing rain, the disturbance lasted until daybreak. For 1½ hours, the forked lightning was replaced by an eerie but wonderful display of continuous and brilliant sheet lightning, but as daylight broke, the clouds moved away and the air became cooler.

The storm, centred on Hoylake, on the Wirral peninsula, where the Open Golf Championship had been underway, left its mark. Before play commenced on the 15th July, it was discovered that lightning had struck the pin on the 5th green and had gouged deep, jagged furrows, radiating from the hole.

Nearly 2 inches of rain was recorded locally, but at Liverpool Airport at Speke the calibrating column was dry.

August 1967: A Wall of Water

Three exceptionally wet days in Lancashire over the 8th, 9th and 10th of August brought severe flooding across the whole county, successive thunderstorms delivering prodigious quantities of rain. Falls exceeded 3 inches in 2 hours in the Forest of Bowland, the central region being deluged with 4.6 inches in just 90 minutes. There was also great havoc in the Downham–Burnley area. The cost of flood damage in the Rossendale Valley alone exceeded half a million pounds and there was massive destruction in the Lune Valley, where Bill Brown of Backsbottom Farm, outside Wray, had a nasty surprise.

On a hot and sultry morning, Bill Brown and neighbour Leonard Richardson were dipping sheep alongside the diminutive river Roeburn. Around noon they heard thunder and it began to rain heavily. At first they ignored the downpour and worked on, unaware of the unfolding drama, one so full of incident that it has become part of local legend.

But everything stops for tea! Not to be denied their cuppa, Bill and Leonard retreated to the farmhouse before returning to complete their work. By this time the, by now, muddy little river had risen by a metre . . . and the duo worked on. Finishing the dipping, they retired for supper.

At around half past five, with the rain still pelting down, Bill saw the river, '. . . it just boiled over the garden wall, like boiling up in a pan.' Realising the danger to his sheep, he and his pal rushed outside and opened the pen gates. Some animals dashed to safety. Others were carried away in the tide of water that surrounded the farmhouse. Then, about 400 metres up the valley, Leonard Richardson saw a spectacle that made his jaw drop.

'Leonard Richardson ran towards the nearby village of Wray to seek help.' August 1967.

A wall of water rushed towards the two men. Leonard raised the alarm and dashed for the footbridge spanning the river, shouting 'Bill, get out! Get out!' In the nick of time, Leonard reached the far bank and turned to see the flimsy structure washed downstream. Bill, meanwhile, had managed to reach the imperilled farmhouse, an island in a sea of flailing water and uprooted trees. Seeing the futility of attempting a rescue single-handed, Leonard ran towards the nearby village of Wray to seek help.

After 30 minutes frantic running, he reached the outskirts of the village and immediately telephoned the fire brigade, directing all available crews towards Backsbottom Farm. This done, he turned his attention to helping the villagers of Wray, most of whom were already removing property to higher ground. One old resident, however, obstinately refused to believe that

A wall of water smashes the cottages in Wray, August 1967.

flooding was imminent. A Roeburn watcher for over 70 years, he confidently predicted 'The river won't get any higher than this.'

This announcement was accompanied by a tremendous roar and, just seconds later, two cottages near the bridge collapsed like a pack of cards. Raging across the village street, the demolishing torrent next assailed a row of homes. Whole tree trunks were smashed into the walls, which were stripped away, furniture from the gaping rooms floating off downstream.

Unprecedented in local history, this infamous flood brought a repair bill costing thousands of pounds, but thankfully nobody was killed. Backsbottom Farm and Bill Brown survived, but the architecture of Wray was forever altered.

14th February 1969: Love in a Cold Climate

Valentine's Day ardours were chilled when up to 10 inches of snow brought most parts of Lancashire to a complete standstill. From the frozen heart of Manchester to isolated villages and farms west of the Pennines, everything with wheels ground to a halt.

Sweeping in over the Fylde coast at 2 am, blizzards deposited a thick blanket of snow, blocking roads and railways and severely disrupting bus and train timetables. Thousands of people were late for work, an RAC spokesman in Manchester declaring an almost complete paralysis. Local airports also felt the strain, ground staff at Manchester and Blackpool battling to open runways.

In Middleton, a 25 vehicle pile-up closed Heywood Old Road as cars and vans slithered and collided on the treacherous road surface. Motorists endured similar chaotic conditions all over the county. In Bolton, on the Bury road, for example, an ambulance carrying a patient was stuck in traffic for three-quarters of an hour.

With champagne languishing in buckets of melted ice, it was indeed a most frustrating day!

Sixties Snippets

1960: Five succeeding depressions crossed Lancashire during July, depressing the sales of ice-cream and firming the resolve of holidaymakers. 'Next year we're going abroad!' Rain fell on all 31 days of the month over the Pennines. Darwen returned a depth of 11.92 inches. August in the county was also exceptionally wet. Ever a resort for making its mark, Blackpool returned a tally of 7 inches of the infuriating liquid in November.

1962: Gales blew off two sails of the famous Marsh Mill windmill at Thornton, near Fleetwood, in December.

1963: In January, one of the two remaining sails on the Marsh Mill windmill was carried away by the wind.

1964: Exceptionally large hailstones belted Burnley on the 18th January.

1968: With clear blue skies for 11.9 hours on the 13th April, Manchester enjoyed its sunniest Good Friday of the century. It did not last! Newspapers on the 5th July reviewed the wettest July day for 80 years – nearly 3 inches fell in two days. A manhole cover in Vine Street, Abbey Hey, was blown 15 ft into the air by storm water and housewives were ankle deep in a noxious brown sludge at Debenham Avenue and Aldham Avenue, Newton Heath, after sewerage pipes burst.

The driest summer for years on the north-west coast left the Lune and its tributaries depressingly low. Fishing for salmon and trout was badly affected.

The late August Bank Holiday weather in Urmston and Stretford was 'temperamental'. Lightning struck and damaged two houses in Budworth Road, Sale. Commenting on the inclemency, one local newspaper chirped 'Lancashire – Colder Than Moscow.'

On the 21st October, with the temperature soaring to 70°F, Manchester had its warmest late October day since records were first compiled in 1877.

1969: After a lengthy dry spell, a succession of Lune spates during September encouraged a hefty run of salmon to enter the river. The long sojourn in the estuary, however, had debilitated the fish and the eating qualities of those grassed were inferior.

THE WEATHER IN
THE SEVENTIES

3rd February 1970: 'Wives To Get 10 Minute Washday Warning'

Inured to the dire MOD predictions about Russian ICBMs and the minimal notice of Armageddon, Manchester housewives nearly missed the eye-catching headlines in the evening newspaper. But this was really important! Never again would they need to rush, peg basket in hand, to rescue the family laundry. A £24,000, 14 ft wide revolving high-tech radar scanner, installed at the top of the Coop Insurance Society Building in Miller Street, would foretell the onset of rain. Frank Ward, meteorologist at the Weather Centre in St Ann's Square trumpeted, 'It will mean that when a housewife rings up on washday we will be able to give her a 10 minute warning of rain and a forecast of whether it will just be a shower or a prolonged spell.' After this announcement, Manchester residents slept more soundly, knowing that come a nuclear bombardment everyone would have dry knickers.

20th February 1970: The Decade Storms In

Gales blowing in excess of 60 mph left a trail of destruction across Lancashire. In Lord Street, Rochdale a freak gust wrecked the top floor of the Wing Wah Chinese restaurant, flinging debris over a distance of 40 yards. Suspecting an explosion, dazed restaurant manager Wong Sang crawled from the wreckage and called the police, saying, 'I heard creaking noises half an hour before the shop front collapsed.' In the Tentercroft area of the town, firemen were summoned to secure a wind-tossed workman's cradle found banging dangerously against the wall of a multi-storey flat, 80 ft from the ground.

Along the coast, high seas battered Blackpool, tossing huge quantities of sand onto the Golden Mile. The tempest delayed the arrival in Liverpool of a Shell supertanker carrying 133,000 tons of Kuwaiti crude oil. She rode out the storm at the Mersey Bar.

1970: Green Sunshine

Evidence was published in the July edition of *Weather*, the highly respected monthly journal of the Royal Meteorological Society, of a distinctly green shaft of sunlight. Mr N. Clarke of Longridge reported two separate sightings of a 'green ray' across a wide valley on clear winter mornings. 'The effect was most remarkable and quite definite. The first "tip of the sun", was definitely green and the light appeared to flood the whole landscape, and to persist for some 2-3 seconds. I may add that on the second occasion I had a colleague with me whom I instructed to watch the first appearance of the sun relative to a fixed landmark. When the flash appeared for the second time I asked him "what colour was it?" and the reply was "green".'

1970: Motorway Badness

Three years of run-off and seepage from the M6 motorway construction site at Tebay had a castastrophic affect on the river Lune. After heavy rainfall, muddy water conditions prevailed for months on end. Conditions were so bad in 1969 that mud and concrete pollution affected the clarity of the water at Halton in Lancashire, over 50 miles downstream, and such was the scouring action of the pollutants that the actual river bed between Lune Bridge and the Sheds was transformed. In 1971 it was estimated that it would be three years before insect life and aquatic plants would reappear in the worst affected parts of the river.

2nd April 1973: Ice-Bomb

A lump of ice weighing in at 22 ounces nearly cleaved the head from university postgraduate Dr Griffiths as he strolled along Burton Road in Manchester. A discerning concretion, it had targeted this official 'lightning watcher' for the Electrical Research Organisation. He emerged unscathed and subjected the ice-bomb to scientific examination, concluding that it was composed of cloud water (not the frozen discharge from some passing aircraft), that it had lost two-thirds of its mass on impact and that no amount of asprin would have cured his headache had the projectile been on target.

July 1975: Bombshells and Spoilt Beer

Ferocious thunderstorms lashed north-east Lancashire on the 14th July, leaving a trail of devastation and flooding. Thunderbolts shorted electricity cables and almost the entire Barnoldswick and Earby areas were blacked out. Lightning struck three houses in Burnley and Brierfield but despite extensive damage no one was injured. Eric Ferguson of Ayr Grove, Burnley was in bed with his wife when his house was hit by a tremendous blast. The explosion demolished the chimney stack, blew out a gas fire in the lounge and burnt out the electrical circuits. 'There was a big flash and a tremendous bang,' said Mr Ferguson. 'It seemed as if the whole house had caved in.'

HOW MUCH PRECIOUS WATER HAVE YOU WASTED TODAY?

North West
Water Authority

Exhortations to save water, 1976.

Only three days later a cloudburst swamped parts of Todmorden and Rossendale. Mudslides up to 3 ft deep engulfed 15 houses in Coronation Terrace at Burnley Road, Portsmouth and there was widespread damage to industrial and commercial property. Licensed premises were particularly badly hit. The Swan Hotel near Suttons lost 1,600 pints of newly delivered beer and in the Bacup and Stacksteads districts the King George VI, the Hare and Hounds, the British Queen, the Waterworks, the Wellington, the Farholme Tavern, the Railway Tavern, the Waterloo and the Queens were all badly affected.

2nd January 1976: Inflated Premiums

Structural damage was reported from almost every county in England, following one of the most severe wind storms this century. The gale claimed at least 23 lives across the UK and sent insurance costs rocketing.

Atmospheric winds gusting at between 150 and 160 knots were strongest over Lancashire at 2100 GMT. Surface speeds exceeded 80 knots, causing widespread damage to property. In Liverpool, a landing stage for the Mersey ferry, recently completed at a cost of £1.25 million, was sunk. The cost to the nation was estimated at £100 million. On the 3rd January, shares fell sharply on the Stock Exchange.

The storm led to flooding along the east coast of England and along the shorelines of Denmark and Holland. In two separate incidents in the Swiss Alps, passengers were left dangling in wind-damaged cable cars.

1976: The Hottest Summer for Years

The summer of this blazing year brought the worst drought conditions in England for nearly 250 years and fuelled the ongoing debate about global warming, fossil fuel emissions, CFCs and ozone depletion, rain forest exploitation and our profilgate use of water. For congenitally welly-booted Lancastrians, the absence of murk was the strongest argument yet against conservation.

For once 'Flaming June' lived up to its reputation, most places in the county totting up a sunshine total of nearly 300 hours. With only ½ inch of rain on Merseyside throughout the whole month, sales of beer and ice-cream rocketed and resorts along the Lancashire coast reported bumper business. On the 31st June, Liverpool became the warmest place in Britain, gasping in a temperature of 86.2°F.

The thermometer nudged even higher on the 1st July, the heatwave stranding hundreds of passengers at Lime Street station in Liverpool. As temperatures soared, points and signalling equipment expanded, jamming all electronic systems. Engineers toiled for two hours with oxyacetylene cutting gear before trains were allowed to continue. With tinder-dry conditions persisting for most of the month, grass fires became a recurring problem. On the 6th July, firemen were called to the Royal Birkdale golf course to hose down a fire alongside one of the fairways and, on the 20th, two popular walkers' routes in the Forest of Bowland were closed by the Lancashire County Council to reduce the risk of fire. As the Government prepared to rush emergency legislation through Parliament to enable water authorities to cope with the drought, one clinical psychologist was predicting that the heatwave could cause a dramatic fall in the birthrate. 'The heat makes men disinclined to initiate any activity,' he said, 'although they feel more sexually aroused.'

During August there was almost dawn to dusk sunshine for the entire month. Dessicated gardens and fields cracked and cereal and vegetable yields were much reduced, causing price rises. With the heat came explosions in insect populations, the abiding memory for some being the sight of millions of ladybirds gorging

100

Trainee high wire act, Anchorsholme Lane, Cleveleys, November 1977. (Blackpool Gazette & Herald)

on the super-abundant hatches of greenfly. Ironically, the last summer bank holiday of the year was wet. Coinciding with the rain came news that the North-West Water Authority planned to erect standpipes in the Rossendale Valley, starting their operation in Bacup. More ironic still were the idiosyncrasies of September – the second wettest in England since 1727.

13th – 14th November 1977: Carpets lifted by the Irish Sea

Fuelled by savage winds, huge seas and storm clouds battered the Lancashire coast, smashing defences, carrying away roads and flooding chalets and homes. Thousands of tons of salt water poured through a breach in the embankment at Crossens near Southport, inundating the Harrogate Way-Skipton Avenue

A flooded Chatsworth Avenue, Fleetwood, November 1977. (Blackpool Gazette & Herald)

Pier disappears – storm damage at Morecambe, November 1977. (Lancashire Evening Post)

housing estate, where scores of families were evacuated. One resident described his ordeal, 'I woke up in the middle of the night thinking the rain was getting pretty hard, and was horrifed to see the Irish Sea going past my house. It came through the floorboards and lifted up our carpets. This morning we found a dead fish in the back garden.'

At Crosby, waves broke through the embankment at the Marine Park, depositing mountains of silt. Liverpool escaped lightly, with few reports of damage, but in Widnes town centre the 75 mph winds toppled a chimney.

After the gales had subsided, scores of curious motorists arrived in Southport to inspect the devastation, ignoring warnings advising of the dangers of two high voltage electricity cables exposed by the storm near Crossens sluice gate. 'These people are putting their own lives in danger purely to sightsee,' lambasted Sefton's Deputy Engineer. 'It is totally irresponsible.'

Seventies Synopsis

1970: Violent thunderstorms swept across the north-west on the 11th June. Overflowing tanks at a sewage works polluted the river Ribble for 4 miles. Hundreds of coarse fish were killed, together with a small number of sea-trout and salmon. On the same day, two schoolboys were struck dead by lightning at Denton, Manchester, where, over a period of just a few minutes, the temperature plunged 13° from a high of 79°F. Manchester Fire Brigade received 179 flooding calls in 90 minutes.

Hurricane force winds clocked 150 mph in the Isle of Man on the 3rd of November. Lancashire took a pounding, with gusts of 73 mph snatching boats from their moorings, toppling chimneys and ripping up trees. Damage was heavy in Salford, Openshaw and Rusholme. Chorley Old Road in Bolton was closed after a 50 ft long wall collapsed.

A weather-memorable year ended with severe icing. Over the Christmas holiday 16 people died on local roads.

1971: As a consequence of low rainfall, fishing on the Lune was the worst for years. In June, conditions were so bad and the smell of undiluted sewage so nauseous that netsmen in the Lune estuary complained to the Public Health Inspector. Ironically, the heavens opened in early October as the season closed, allowing the massed shoals of fish in the estuary to enter the river. Some of the ascending salmon were estimated at over 20 lbs.

1972: As people were rousing for work at 6.55 am on the 7th March, an earthquake rocked parts of Lancashire. In Leyland,

Accrington, Walton-le-Dale, Rawtenstall and Heywood, houses trembled, walls and ceilings cracked and furniture rattled. At the Burgess Becker School in Harpurhey, Manchester, a collection of crockery assembled for an Easter fair was smashed to pieces, and in Bacup a chimney came crashing down.

Despite the advent of extremely wet weather in spring, a general famine of water during the rest of the year reduced the depth reading on the Lune's Caton gauge to zero in September.

1973: An ice block weighing in at over 3 lbs was reported to have fallen on Withington, Manchester, on the 2nd April.

During June, 'rainstorms of some magnitude swept through the county, leaving some distruption in their wake but miraculously avoiding the catchment areas of the Lune and Wenning rivers, whose water gauges remained at zero.'

1974: The headwaters of the Mersey at Kinder Downfall, Derbyshire, dried up in April in drought conditions. In the same month the lowlands of Lancashire had a total absence of rain.

1975: On Sunday, 3rd August, a temperature of 87°F was recorded in the Billington area, the highest since 30th July 1901.

1976: Home consumption of suntan products soared in June and July. Temperatures along the Lancashire coast reached 89.6°F on the 30th June. Liverpool and St Helens recorded 90°F on the same day. During the following week, sunbathers in Blackpool peeled off in their thousands when thermometers topped the 90s.

1978: 'Brass monkey' conditions in Manchester during the first eight days of July depressed sales of shorts and bikinis. Temperatures remained in the 50s throughout.

1979: During the night of the 28th/29th November, sand-ladened rain peppered Blackpool.

THE WEATHER IN
THE EIGHTIES

13th and 14th December 1981: Cold Comfort

Roads were blocked, villages cut off and scores of vehicles abandoned in some of the worse blizzard conditions in 30 years. Snow storms raged across the county, fuelled by 40 mph winds gusting up to gale force in places. The Rossendale and Craven areas took the brunt of the onslaught and, by dawn on the 14th, all roads from Burnley to the Rossendale Valley were closed to traffic. Schools throughout north-east Lancashire were badly affected, thousands of children in Burnley gleefully dusting off their sledges after they had been given the day off.

Licensed hostelries had mixed fortunes. One of Pendle's most isolated pubs – the Herders, on the moor road between Laneshaw Bridge and Haworth – was cut off and had little custom. It was a different story in the lounge of the Waggoners Inn on Manchester Road in Burnley. Stranded by the atrocious weather, 40 travellers snuggled up for the night, spirits bolstered by the kindness of publicans Roy and Ann Kenyon. Mrs Kay Turner of Barnoldswick said, 'Conditions were chaotic and frightening. The howling wind was blowing the snow into huge drifts. We got into the Waggoners at 9 pm and Mr and Mrs Kenyon gave us a great welcome and provided hot soup and sandwiches.'

Speed arresters on Summit Tunnel at Todmorden end, between Littleborough and Todmorden, December 1981. (M A Bunn)

Huge drifts up to 10 ft deep blocked the road at Crown Point between Bacup and Burnley and the Grane Road between Haslingden and Blackburn was also closed. Roads were also impassable in the Ormskirk area and 27 schools were closed in Liverpool.

12th and 13th January 1982: Strike While It's Cold

On the 12th January, black ice, freezing fog and an untimely rail strike brought chaotic misery for Merseyside commuters. Treacherous roads and visibility as low as 10 yards accounted for a spate of accidents and two people died on the M6. With traffic down to a crawl on the M62, thousands of Barnsley football supporters missed the League Cup quarter final match with Liverpool at Anfield.

High Wyre. East side of St Michael's, 1983. (Blackpool Gazette & Herald)

On the following day, despite the dense fog, the area escaped the predicted road chaos, many motorists heeding the appeal to share cars.

1st February 1983: Tidal Raise

Hurricane force winds gusting at up to 83 mph increased tide levels so much in Fleetwood dock that the fishing boat *Lady Peta* was lifted onto the quayside. Docklands and resorts along the entire Lancashire coast were pounded by mountainous seas and millions of pounds worth of damage was caused.

In Southport, 100 homes were swamped when the river Crossens overflowed. Part of Bootle's Alexandra Dock was smashed by huge waves and caterpillar-tracked vehicles had to be brought in to clear giant rocks and boulders washed from the sea defences at Seaforth. In one of the most dramatic incidents of a drama filled day, Merseyside firemen and frogmen saved a ship from sinking in a Liverpool dry dock, whose gates had been buckled by the storm.

The winds brought further terror inland. In Haydock, a fleeing family miraculously escaped injury as the winds sheared off the gable end of their home and, in Warrington, the Ferry Inn at Penketh, was flooded to a depth of several feet when the river Mersey burst its banks.

14th January 1984: Air Line Fractures

Reaching storm force 10, the worst gales on Merseyside for 20 years caused a number of broken arms and legs. Two wind-blown pedestrians suffered shattered limbs on Liverpool's Pier Head, where, at its height, the wind velocity reached 94 mph.

Chimney stacks and trees toppled like nine pins and, in St Helens, brave firemen scaled the roof of St Teresa's church at Newtown to lop off the damaged top 4 ft of the tower, which hung precariously over a footway. The emergency services were also in action in Formby, where the railway station was cordoned off to reduce the danger of injury from falling masonry and roof tiles. Further north, a woman and her four teenage children fled to safety when the gable end of their Southport home collapsed.

Motorist Norman Simmons had a remarkable escape from death in Allerton. A huge beech tree toppled onto the roof of his car as he drove along Druids Cross Road. He emerged from the written-off vehicle without a scratch.

With plaster of Paris in great demand, scores of out-patient appointments had to be cancelled at local hospitals.

'It huffed and it puffed . . .' Gales damaged the 17th-century Thatched House in Roseacre Road, Wharles, near Kirkham, in January 1984. (Lancashire Evening Post)

12th and 13th and 14th January 1987: Iceberg on the Mersey

With biting winter temperatures threatening to crack thermometers, seawater froze at Meols, and ice floes formed in the shipping channel near the entrance to the Manchester Ship Canal. A numb keeper at Eastham Locks stuttered, 'I don't think many people down here can remember it happening before.' Hundreds of Merseyside pensioners suffered from hypothermia – one old lady died in St Helens – the terrible weather being exacerbated by a power cut in Liverpool, which left 1,500 homes without power.

At higher altitudes, conditions on the A58 road to Rochdale and the M62 Trans-Pennine route were described as atrocious. Diesel fuel froze solid and scores of lorries and hundreds of cars were left stranded.

Things were bad but we could count our blessings. In Leningrad, the temperature fell to −31°F. 'Never in the annals of the Leningrad weather service – and meteorologists have been working here since 1743 – have such low temperatures been registered for several days running,' said a spokesman. And Norwegian doctors warned people against drinking hot beverages immediately after coming in from the cold. Several incidents of cracking tooth enamel had been reported!

Thankfully, the harsh conditions petered out and a thaw set in, just as British Rail sent its Bielhack self-propelled rotary snow blower to England from its Inverness base.

Eighties Headlines

1980: After the driest spring in parts of Lancashire this century (no measurable rain fell for 48 consecutive days in Burnley in

Adam's ale in flooded bar of the White Lion, Halton, near Lancaster, October 1980. (Lancashire Evening Post)

April and May) heavy rain brought flooding to many parts of the county on the 27th October. Police set up a special incident room to monitor problems in the Gisburn, Barnoldswick, Clitheroe and Longridge areas, where many roads were closed. Pendle Water broke its banks in Barley and flooded the picnic ground, and a huge lake formed in front of Barden Lane Bridge. Hundreds of acres of farmland around the village of Ribchester were under several feet of water.

1981: Ringway Airport had a record 24 hour deluge of rain on 5th and 6th August, measuring 3.8 inches.

1982: On the 15th January, following the coldest winter night since 1895, the sea froze at Southport and ice floes formed on the Mersey. British Rail services were 'bedevilled by frozen points

'He took a dive, Ref!' Farm worker Alec Western going for goal at the Bottomdale Road pitch, Slyne, near Lancaster, November 1980. (Lancashire Evening Post)

and equipment.' Iced-up piping kept scores of diesel units in their sidings and services between Liverpool and St Helens and Liverpool and Warrington were cancelled.

One of the quickest thaws on record on the 17th January released millions of gallons of water, bringing flood misery to thousands of Merseysiders. There were over 2,000 separate flood incidents in Liverpool alone.

1983: Scientists spent three weeks on an exposed and elevated site at Chew reservoir east of Manchester. In analysing water droplets they found acid concentrations ten times greater than those in samples from other Pennine areas. The droplets also contained large amounts of aluminium, titanium and particles of fly ash.

A slurp at the oasis. Three regulars combat the drought in August 1984. The spring-fed stone trough at the Golden Lion pub at Higher Wheelton, near Chorley, never dried up. (Lancashire Evening Post)

Haweswater, 11th July 1984. Only 13% left in the wettest place in England. (Lancashire Evening Post)

1984: 'COSTA DEL CROSBY' trumpeted the local newspaper as coastal temperatures on the 24th April reached 70°F. Ice-cream sellers did a roaring trade in Southport as a weather expert stuck out his neck, declaring brashly, 'it looks as though it's going to last forever.'

1985: Destructive electrical storms left a trail of havoc across Lancashire on the 27th July. Power lines in all parts of the county were short circuited and in Orrell, near Wigan, worshippers at St James' church had an amazing escape when a thunderbolt missed them by just 10 ft.

1986: Dr John Lee from the Department of Botany at the University of Manchester published scientific evidence showing

A wet night in Black Bull Lane, Fulwood, October 1987. (Lancashire Evening Post)

In the swim. Leyland town centre, January 1988. (Lancashire Evening Post)

that, over the past century, acid rain has destroyed vast tracts of Pennine bog moss. In one experiment, he transplanted Welsh moss to a moorland site above Manchester. The moss died from a surfeit of nitrogen.

Unannounced to the world on the 26th April, the nuclear catastrophe at Chernobyl released a radioactive cloud that contaminated half of Europe. Carried on the prevailing winds, some of the deadly material washed to earth in raindrops, polluting much of Scotland and England. Despite initial assurances from the authorities that the risks to health were negligible, tests by the National Radiological Protection Board found that radioactive contaminants in ground samples were up to ten times higher in the north of England than in the south.

People in Lancashire were warned not to drink rainwater, there was constant monitoring of milk and some farmers were banned from sending carcases to market.

1987: Six Liverpool seamen were airlifted to safety in gale force winds after their tug *Wallasey* was grounded by a giant wave off Formby on the 27th March. Merseyside took a pounding and local fire brigades made a number of dramatic rescues.

Calmed by the bedtime assurances of Michael Fish on the 16th October, the nation slept soundly, confident in the knowledge that weather ships, satellites, banks of sophisticated computers and posses of meteorological boffins were keeping a watchful eye. But everything was on the blink! Lurking in the English Channel, a massive depression unleashed hurricane force winds against southern England, demolishing hundreds of homes and factories, smashing cars and boats to smithereens, uprooting millions of trees and leaving scores of people dead. The storm passed out into the North Sea and left Lancashire largely unscathed.

INTO THE NINETIES

1990: The Manchester Myth

For over a century Manchester has been under a cloud, its reputation for damp streets and sodden roofs preserved under a sunproof mantle of smoke being the butt of more jokes than Ken Dodd's tax returns! But the jibes, originating, it is said, from 1880, when the city was the venue for the first Test Match in history to be entirely washed out, are now unfair. Who said so? The international authority on the science of meteorology, Lancaster Professor Gordon Manley, who addressed the Manchester Luncheon Club on the 23rd June.

'There is probably no place in the world where man has done so much damage to the climate', said Professor Manley, blaming atmospheric pollution, building density and reduced rates of evaporation for the city's former dour image. 'But things are now much improved and I congratulate Manchester on its effort and accomplishment in eliminating so much of the smoke I remember in my youth.'

The sun shone during the professor's visit from his Cambridgeshire home but he had come well prepared, the mysterious bulge in his jacket pocket secreting a state of the art Pak-a-Mac.

March 1993: Wind Kill Factor

Pennine rainfall figures showed an increase of 170–180 per cent during one of the most abysmal months ever for Lancashire sheep farmers. Incessant driving rain, interspersed with sleet and snow flurries, killed scores of newborn lambs on upland farms. The fatalities were worsened by the poor condition of pregnant ewes, weakened by high winds and excessive spring showers.

14th March 1994: Wind Cheaters

Gusting at up to 60 mph, gales swept Lancashire, causing structural damage and a spate of minor injuries. In Farnworth, near Bolton, resolute pensioner, William Blundell, 71, propped up his damaged garage roof for nearly an hour to prevent it being blown onto the top of his new Mercedes car. Helped by his son Brian, he protected the vehicle until the fire brigade arrived. 'I've only had the car two weeks,' panted Mr Blundell, 'and it was my life's ambition to own a Mercedes, I didn't want it dented or scratched. One side of the garage was blown about 10 yards up the garden and the rest would have come down on the car if I hadn't held it up.'

Naughty Nineties

1990: Blowing with hurricane force, a storm left a trail of destruction across southern and western counties of England, causing damage estimated at £2,081 million. Shuttle flights were delayed between Ringway and London and a power failure wreaked havoc at Piccadilly railway station in Manchester.

Liverpool recorded its highest ever tide on the 26th February.

1993: On the 4th January, police recovered the body of a 10 year old boy, who had fallen through an ice-covered pond at Walkden, Salford.

Blackpool Promenade, July 1990. (Lancashire Evening Post)

As firemen fought to rescue flood-stranded householders in Windsor on the 13th October, Blackpool was 'being seriously flooded by sunshine.' Shirt-sleeved visitors strolled on the promenade, donkeys ambled on the beach and it was business as usual on the Golden Mile. 'We've had only two days written off by rain in the last three weeks,' said a tourist department spokesman. 'We're enjoying autumn at its best.'

Violent gales battered Britain on the 9th December, causing at least 13 fatalities. A 40 year old demolition worker died in Urmston, Manchester, when he was hit by a steel-framed shed.

1994: Manchester City's match against Ipswich was abandoned after 39 minutes on the 3rd January because water made the pitch unplayable.

Potty about his car. Gales brought motorist David Freear a surprise passenger on 3rd February 1994. He stopped at traffic lights near the King's Arms Hotel in Market Street, Morecambe, and a chimney pot smashed through his windscreen. (Lancashire Evening Post)

Mid-morning blizzards on the M62 were so bad on the 2nd February that police came within 20 minutes of closing this so-called 'snow-proof' motorway. On the 23rd February, blizzards brought travel chaos to the county, drifting snow adding to the problems of snowplough and gritting crews.

Weather experts confirmed in September that Britain's sultry summer had brought the highest number of lightning deaths for a decade. 'It's difficult to predict if it heralds a climatic trend,' said an expert.

Bathed in tropical air from the south-west, the country enjoyed the mildest November since records began in 1659.

April cower. Typical spring bank holiday weather by the Mersey. (Liverpool Daily Post & Echo)

Lashed by Christmas storms, South Wales endured 7 inches of rain in just 3 days. Many Lancashire rivers were swollen and a 38 year old canoeist from Harpurhey, Manchester died when he was thrown out of his craft in white water on the river Goyt at Brabyns Park, Marple Bridge, Stockport. On the 28th December, Blackburn's home game with Leeds was called off due to a waterlogged pitch.

1995: On the 10th January, gale force winds blew a 32 year old oil rig worker into Liverpool Bay. Despite an extensive search his body was not found. 'Cantona Outwits Force Ten', announced a newspaper headline on the same day, following Manchester United's 2–0 win at the gale-lashed Bramall Lane, Sheffield, ground. The weather omens were good even before the kick-off, the wind 'filling the Manchester United goal with pre-match balloons.'

Little-anticipated blizzards (forecasters were again woefully late with their warnings) swept across the region on the 26th and 27th January bringing total paralysis. More than 5,000 motorists were stranded on the M62 alone. In the wake of snow came February floods and dozens of properties in Rossendale were inundated.

Clocks went forward in March – generally a mild month – but unseasonal snowfalls put all thoughts of spring on ice – a substance much in evidence during a generally chilly April which saw penetrating frosts even after the Easter break. We consoled ourselves on hearing reports from China on the 19th of the month, when 37 people died and £20 million pounds worth of damage was caused by a combination of rainstorms, tornadoes and hailstones. 'In Huizhou, we had hailstones as big as basketballs,' said an official. 'The heaviest we found in Zhaoqing City; it weighed 33 lbs.'

After a freak week of 70°F plus temperatures and uninterrupted blue skies between the 29th April and the 6th May winter returned to the county. Thermometers plunged a full 40° and Crosby became the coldest place in the country with a low of 27°F.

Glossary of Common Weather Terms

Altitude: Height above sea level.

Anticyclone: An area of high pressure bringing fine weather.

Atmosphere: A gaseous envelope surrounding the earth.

Aurora borealis: The 'Northern Lights', a spectacular heavenly phenomenon producing brilliant displays of colour, caused by the atmospheric disturbance of oxygen and nitrogen by electrons and protons radiating from the sun.

Ball lightning: A suspended sphere of radiating energy, explained as an electrical dust cloud, a slow-burning admixture of air and carbon or an ionised mass of gas.

Barometer: An instrument for measuring atmospheric pressure.

Clouds: Condensed water vapour.

Drought: A prolonged absence of precipitation.

Fog: Clouds of condensing water vapour, resulting from the interaction of warm and cold air.

Front: The boundary between two masses of air of differing densities or temperatures.

Frost: Frozen dew or water vapour.

Gale: Wind measured in velocity between 34 and 40 knots.

Glaze: Rain which freezes on contact with the ground.

Hail: A form of precipitation consisting of ice pellets of more than 1 cm (0.39 inches) in diameter.

Hurricane: Wind measured in velocity in excess of 64 knots.

Lightning: A flash of energy produced by an electrical discharge between clouds or between clouds and the ground.

Mist: An increase in water droplet concentrations in the air, resulting in decreased visibility.

Rain: Liquid precipitation whose individual droplets measure up to 6 mm (0.24 inches) in diameter.

Rainbow: Optical phenomena occurring when sunlight is refracted into spectral colours by shower clouds. The larger the raindrops, the more intense the rainbow.

Sleet: Form of precipitation consisting of a mixture of melting snow and rain.

Snow: Frozen flakes of ice in the shape of six-pointed stars.

Thermometer: Instrument for measuring temperature.

Thunder: The audible consequences of air particle compression and collision in air vacuums created by lightning activity.

Thunderstorm: Onset of rapidly rising moist air, attended by heavy rain, thunder and lightning.

Tornado: A violent columnar spiral of wind travelling at great speed.

Wind: The process of pressure equalisation: air moving from high pressure to low pressure.

Index